Wedding in Paris

A Romantic Musical Play

Vera Caspary

A Samuel French Acting Edition

FOUNDED 1830

SAMUELFRENCH-LONDON.CO.UK
SAMUELFRENCH.COM

Music and Lyrics Copyright © 1955 by Keith Prowse & Co. Ltd
Copyright © (Acting Edition) 1956 by Samuel French Ltd
All Rights Reserved

WEDDING IN PARIS is fully protected under the copyright laws of the British Commonwealth, including Canada, the United States of America, and all other countries of the Copyright Union. All rights, including professional and amateur stage productions, recitation, lecturing, public reading, motion picture, radio broadcasting, television and the rights of translation into foreign languages are strictly reserved.

ISBN 978-0-573-08032-6

www.samuelfrench-london.co.uk

www.samuelfrench.com

FOR AMATEUR PRODUCTION ENQUIRIES

UNITED KINGDOM AND WORLD EXCLUDING NORTH AMERICA

plays@SamuelFrench-London.co.uk

020 7255 4302/01

Each title is subject to availability from Samuel French, depending upon country of performance.

CAUTION: Professional and amateur producers are hereby warned that WEDDING IN PARIS is subject to a licensing fee. Publication of this play does not imply availability for performance. Both amateurs and professionals considering a production are strongly advised to apply to the appropriate agent before starting rehearsals, advertising, or booking a theatre. A licensing fee must be paid whether the title is presented for charity or gain and whether or not admission is charged.

The professional rights in this play are controlled by Samuel French Ltd, 52 Fitzroy Street, London, W1T 5JR.

No one shall make any changes in this title for the purpose of production. No part of this book may be reproduced, stored in a retrieval system, or transmitted in any form, by any means, now known or yet to be invented, including mechanical, electronic, photocopying, recording, videotaping, or otherwise, without the prior written permission of the publisher. No one shall upload this title, or part of this title, to any social media websites.

The right of Vera Caspary to be identified as author of this work has been asserted by her in accordance with Section 77 of the Copyright, Designs and Patents Act 1988

WEDDING IN PARIS

Presented by George and Alfred Black at The London Hippodrome on the 3rd April 1954, with the following cast of characters :

(in the order of their appearance)

CHURCHILL, a newspaper boy	*Brian Leslie*
ALICE DOBSON	*Maidie Andrews*
ANGY, her daughter	*Susan Swinford*
THE MAYOR OF HITCHEMUP	*Sydney Arnold*
MR AIKEN	*Bill Clothier*
MRS AIKEN	*Maureen Shelley*
PAUL CHANDLER	*Jeff Warren*
THE CHIEF STEWARD	*Derek Warner*
MARCELLE THIBAULT	*Evelyn Laye*
MRS PILCHARD	*Joan Emney*
JACQUES DEVALLÉE	*Anton Walbrook*
DIXWOOD AIKEN	*Ryck Rydon*
MAID	*Alissande White*
LA TOULOUSE	*Maidie Andrews*
WAITER	*Chester Gordon*
BUTLER	*Philip Jay*

Dancers

RESIDENTS OF HITCHEMUP, PASSENGERS, CUSTOMS OFFICERS, PORTERS, TOURISTS, REPORTERS, PARISIANS, WEDDING GUESTS

The play directed by CHARLES HICKMAN
Settings designed by THÉA NEU

SYNOPSIS OF SCENES

ACT I

SCENE 1 Angy's Front Porch, Hitchemup, Saskatchewan
SCENE 2 The ship's rail, S.S. *Queen Anne*
SCENE 3 The sun terrace, S.S. *Queen Anne*
SCENE 4 The ship's rail, S.S. *Queen Anne*
SCENE 5 The sun terrace, S.S. *Queen Anne*
SCENE 6 Another part of the ship's rail, S.S. *Queen Anne*
SCENE 7 The Customs Shed, Le Havre

ACT II

SCENE 1 Marcelle's Garden. Morning
SCENE 2 A Paris Street
SCENE 3 A Paris Boulevard
SCENE 4 Jacques' Library
SCENE 5 Marcelle's Garden. Evening
SCENE 6 Outside the Cathedral, Paris
SCENE 7 Inside the Cathedral, Paris

MUSIC

ACT I

No.	1	Overture	
No.	2	Melos	
No.	3	"A Wedding in Paris"	Angy and Chorus
No.	4	"Angy's Farewell"	Angy and Chorus
No.	5	"It's News"	Marcelle and Paul
No.	6	"The French Lesson"	Angy and Paul
No.	6a	"In a Cosy Corner of the Upper Deck"	Chorus
No.	7	Ship Ballet	Dancers
No.	8	"The Young in Heart"	Jacques and Chorus
No.	9	Fairy Tale and "Lovely Lady of the Sands"	Jacques
No.	9a	Reprise. "Lovely Lady of the Sands"	Chorus
No.	10	Waltz Ballet and Melos	Dancers
No.	11	"The Simple Things of Life"	Marcelle
No.	11a	Melos	
No.	11b	Melos	
No.	12	"It Only Took a Moment"	Angy and Paul
No.	12a	Melos and Choir	Chorus
No.	13	Harbour Ballet	Dancers and Chorus
No.	14	"I Have Nothing to Declare but Love"	Paul, Angy and Chorus
No.	15	Finale, Act I	Chorus
No.	16	Intermission	Orchestra

ACT II

No.	17	Paris Ballet	Dancers
No.	18	"The Streets of Gay Paree"	Chorus
No.	19	"A Man is a Man is a Man"	Marcelle and Reporters
No.	20	"Tourist Song"	La Toulouse, Mrs Pilchard and Chorus
No.	21	"How Do I Know it's Love?"	Angy, Girls and Dancers
No.	22	"I Must Have Been Crazy"	Paul
No.	23	"Strike Another Match"	Jacques
No.	24	Pink Ballet	Dancers
No.	25	"In the Pink"	Marcelle and Chorus
No.	26	[This number is cut]	
No.	27	Melos	Orchestra
No.	27a	Reprise. "It Only Took a Moment"	Paul
No.	28	Finale. Act II	Chorus
No.	29	Melos	Full Company

Applications for a licence to perform this play by amateurs must be made to us, or to our authorized agents, giving the following particulars:

 Title of the play
 Name of the town
 Name of the theatre or hall
 The maximum seating capacity of the place of performance
 The number of performances it is intended to give
 The dates of the performances
 The name of the society

On receipt of these particulars we will quote the terms upon which a licence to perform the play will be granted.

SAMUEL FRENCH LTD
26 Southampton Street
Strand, London, W.C.2

The Vocal Score is published, and copies may be obtained from us.

The correct costumes and wigs used in the production of this play may be obtained from Messrs CHARLES H. Fox Ltd, 184 High Holborn, W.C.1 or from Fashion Hire Ltd, 7 Short's Gardens, London, W.C.2

This version of *Wedding in Paris* is a revision of the original professional production, made specially to meet the requirements of Amateur Operatic Societies.

WEDDING IN PARIS

MUSIC

OVERTURE No. 1

ACT I

SCENE I

Angy's Front Porch, Hitchemup, Saskatchewan

The porch and front door of a small white wooden house is L. *Opposite is the General Store and the backcloth depicts other houses in the town and a stretch of wheatfields. There are tree wings above and below the house-pieces* R *and* L. *On one pillar of the porch is a sign that reads* " Dobson School of Theatre Arts " ; *on the other pillar hangs a sign,* " Fresh Eggs and Milk for Sale ". *Two wicker chairs are set side by side* R *of the porch steps.*

MELOS No. 2

When the CURTAIN *rises, the stage is empty.* CHURCHILL, *a young newspaper boy, rushes on up* R, *and runs to the porch* L. *He wears overalls and carries a bundle of newspapers.*

CHURCHILL [*shouting*] Mrs Dobson, Mrs Dobson. [*He knocks on the front door*]

ALICE DOBSON *enters from the house* L. *She is a nice-looking woman in her forties. She has a preoccupied air and carries a wedding dress over her arm.*

[*He takes a paper from his bundle*] Here's your paper, Mrs Dobson.
ALICE. Oh, good morning, Churchill.
CHURCHILL. Angy's picture's in it.
ALICE. Is it ? [*She calls into the house*] Angy. Angy.
CHURCHILL [*showing her the paper*] Here, on the first page. Right under the Governor-General's horse. [*He hands the paper to Alice and moves down the verandah steps to* R *of them*]
ALICE. What an honour ! [*She calls into the house*] Hurry, dear. [*She moves down the verandah steps to* L *of them*]

ANGY *bounces out of the house. She wears pyjamas and is still sleepy, but shows herself an enchanting creature ; at the age when everything is vitally important. Now she bubbles with eagerness. Life is rosy. She is aged nineteen.*

ANGY [*crossing to* C] Bon jour, Maman. How's my French accent today ?
ALICE. Not dressed yet ? Have you forgotten what day it is ?
CHURCHILL [*staring hard at Angy*] I haven't. [*He giggles*]
ALICE [*sternly*] Churchill !

CHURCHILL *exits up* L *above the house. The music fades.*

[*She moves* LC] Look, you're in the morning paper.
ANGY [*moving to Alice and taking the paper from her*] What does it say ? [*She sits on the* R *chair and reads*] " Local Girl off to Paris Troth."
ALICE [*sitting on the chair* L *of Angy*] Right on the front page.
ANGY [*giggling*] As if everybody in town didn't know. [*She reads*] " Angela Dobson, daughter of the distinguished . . . "
ALICE. You can read it on the train. I'll put it in your overnight bag. Hurry now . . .
ANGY. But listen to this part of it. [*She reads*] " Her engagement was announced the day of Dixwood Aiken's departure for Paris where he is a valued employee of International Grain and Cereal Company." Have you ever heard anything more romantic ?
ALICE [*rising*] Hurry ! [*She starts towards the door to pack the wedding dress*]

1

ANGY [*rising*] Wait, Mother. [*She puts the paper on the chair and moves to* R *of Alice*] Don't put my wedding dress away yet. I want to wish on it.

ALICE. Wish on a wedding dress ? It's the new moon you wish on or the first star or a load of hay.

ANGY [*reverently taking the dress and moving down* C] I wish on everything. [*She murmurs*] Oh, please, let my wedding be as wonderful as my dream.

ALICE. Don't be such a child, child. You're almost twenty. Now run along and forget all about the dream.

" A WEDDING IN PARIS "   No. 3

ANGY *and* CHORUS

ALICE *exits into the house* L.

ANGY [*speaking over the music*] Forget! I'll never in my life forget—
[*she sings*] A wedding comes once in a lifetime
That's how I've been told it should be.
And this is a chance in a lifetime,
When somebody said " Marry me ".
I hope for the loveliest wedding
As lovely as my wedding gown.
A plain country girl though I be,
Imagine anything so wonderfully exciting happening
To a plain country bumpkin like me.

A wedding in Paris, I'm going to be married,
In love and in Paris, how grand to be married,
I'm sure ev'ry girl would agree.
The sun will be shining, the birds will be singing,
And from Notre Dame all the bells will be ringing,
No wonder my heart wants to sing.
I could be a bride there,
One morning in May,
He'll be by my side there, and folks will say,
" Oh, what a happy pair ".
A wedding in Paris, I'm going to be married,
And over a threshold I'm going to be carried,
The happiest bride I will be.
Ah, *oui*, there'll be
A wedding in Paris for me.

ANGY *exits into the house* L.

The HITCHEMUP CITIZENS *enter in great excitement* R *and* L. *With them is the* MAYOR, *a stout man who carries his dignity like a load of Saskatchewan corn. Young people in the crowd carry cards on poles with the signs,* " Good Luck, Angy ", " Come Back, Angy " *and* " Bless Our Angy ". *Also with the crowd are* CHURCHILL *and* MR *and* MRS AIKEN.

CHORUS.   A wedding in Paris
A wedding in Paris
A wedding in Paris
A wedding in Paris
A wedding in Paris
A wedding in Paris there'll be.

During the following chorus ALICE *enters from the house* L *and stands on the porch.* MR *and* MRS AIKEN *sit complacently in the chairs* R *of the porch steps.*

SCENE 1 WEDDING IN PARIS

Angy Dobson's off to Paris,
Angy Dobson's on her way,
Angy Dobson's off to Paris,
For her happy wedding day.
We'll be dancing in the village,
There'll be wedding cake and beer,
Though we cannot go to Paris
We will celebrate it here.
Yes, it's Angy and Dix we will drink to,
We will drink to, we will drink to.
Best of luck, best of luck, we will drink to,
Angy Dobson's off to Paris
Angy's going to wed her man
And in Paris they will hear
Of Hitchemup, Saskatchewan.

The CHORUS *splits up into dramatic groups as they gather to listen to the* MAYOR *who mounts the steps of the porch.*

MAYOR. Just a moment! Just a moment! First of all, folks, it gives me great pleasure to introduce a citizen who has done more than any other ...

AIKEN *rises and comes forward.*

AIKEN. Thank you, folks—it gives me pleasure on this auspicious ...
MAYOR [*moving to* L *of Aiken*] Sit down, Mr Aiken, your name hasn't been mentioned.

Everyone laughs. AIKEN, *somewhat flattened, resumes his seat.*

[*He moves to* C] Folks, I'd like you to meet none other than the famous little lady whose Hamlet took the First Prize among the six-month calves at the Country Fair. [*He indicates Alice*]

Everyone applauds.

AIKEN. Let Mrs Dobson speak for herself.
MAYOR. Now, now, don't be a sorehead just because your calf only got a Second Prize.

Everyone applauds.

[*He bows to Alice*] I yield to the lady.
ALICE [*at the top of the porch steps*] If only my late husband had lived to see this day. With our beautiful little girl—excuse me for bragging ...

The others murmur " That's all right ".

MAYOR. No need to be modest.
MRS AIKEN. And what about the bridegroom?
MAYOR [*moving to* L *of Mrs Aiken*] Spoken like a true mother, Mrs Aiken. Here's another little lady that has a right to be proud. [*He moves down* C] Her son's not only making the name of Hitchemup, Saskatchewan, famous in Paris, France, but what's more important, after a year away from home——
MRS AIKEN. Sixteen months.
MAYOR. —sixteen months away from our blue skies and clean Canadian air—[*he crosses to a group of girls* R] Dixwood Aiken has not been lured by the painted women of Europe——

The GIRLS *giggle.*

—but has remained loyal to his childhood sweetheart——

A train whistle is heard off in the distance.

ALICE [*calling frantically into the house*] Angy!
MAYOR. —a fine, clean, true-blue Hitchemup girl.

Everyone applauds.

ANGY *enters from the house. She wears a smart little travelling suit and hat and has a shiny new bag on her arm.*

CROWD [ad lib.] Hey, Angy! Good luck, kid—have fun. Speech! Speech, Angy.

    ANGY *moves down* C, *but the* MAYOR, *moving* R *of Angy, gets in ahead.* ALICE *moves to* L *of Angy and stands nervously fidgeting for her to go.*

MAYOR. And now I wish to introduce a girl who . . .
MAN. Cut it out, we all know her.
CROWD [ad lib.] Speech!
ANGY. All I can say is that I must be the happiest girl in the world . . .

    The train whistle off sounds nearer.

ALICE. We'd better be getting down to the station, Angy.
AIKEN [*rising*] Have 'em hold the train. [*He resumes his seat*]
MAYOR. Tell 'em it's my instructions.

    The STATION MASTER *exits up* L *above the house.*

WOMAN. What about her present?
OTHERS } [*together*] { Yeh—wait—the wedding present.
MAYOR }   { Hey, Lana! [*He beckons* R *and steps back*]

    A WOMAN R *pushes* LANA *forward.* LANA *is a shy little girl. The* WOMAN *whispers to Lana and thrusts an envelope into her hand.* LANA *runs to* R *of Angy.*

LANA. To our dearest Angy from all her friends in her home town. [*She gives the envelope to Angy*]

    Everyone applauds.

ANGY. Thank you, Lana. [*She bends down and kisses Lana*]

    LANA *runs and rejoins the Woman* R.

And thank you all.
CROWD [ad lib.] Open it. See what you got. Will you be surprised?

    Two GIRLS, *giggling, run forward to* R *and* L *of Angy.*

TWO GIRLS [*together*] Well, open it.

    There is an air of excitement and silence as ANGY *opens the envelope. She looks at the contents, thoroughly shocked and deeply stirred. The* CROWD *watches intently.*

ONE GIRL. Do you like it?

    The two GIRLS *retire.*

ANGY [*turning to Alice*] Look, Mother, a ticket on the S.S. **Queen Anne**, First Class.
ALICE. Angy!
MAYOR [*moving down* R] Think we'd let a girl from Hitchemup travel Third Class?
ANGY. Why is everyone so wonderful to me?
CHURCHILL [*moving to* R *of Angy*] We love you, Angy.
MAYOR. It was my idea.
WOMAN. The whole town chipped in.
CHURCHILL [*moving* RC] I gave my comic book money.
LANA [*moving to* R *of Churchill*] And my ice cream dimes.

    CHURCHILL *and* LANA *fight. Two* WOMEN *separate them.*

MRS AIKEN. Sheer extravagance!

    Two GIRLS *move to* R *and* L *of Angy.*

TWO GIRLS [*together*] Like it, Angy?
ANGY. Like it!
TWO GIRLS [*together*] She likes it.

    The two GIRLS *resume their places in the crowd.*

SCENE 2   WEDDING IN PARIS   5

ANGY.   Imagine me, on the *Queen Anne*! Like a movie star. [*Tears flow a little*] Only better.   <u>MUSIC</u>
[*She starts to break down*]   You shouldn't have done it.
TWO BOYS [*together*]   Cheer up, Angy.   It couldn't happen to a nicer person.
                                                The train whistle off sounds much nearer.
ALICE.   Hurry, dear.
ANGY.   Honestly. I don't know how to make a speech, all I can say is——

                                  " ANGY'S FAREWELL "   No. 4
                                       ANGY *and* CHORUS

ANGY.   My heart is so full at this moment,
                At parting, that's how it should be.
                Could I have one wish at this moment,
                I'd wish you were coming with me.
                I'll never forget all your kindness,
                I'll always remember this day.
                I know you'll be thinking of me,
                [*She turns away to shed a tear*]
                Just thinking how happy I'll be.
                             During the chorus, ANGY *runs from group to group, saying good-bye.*
CHORUS.   A wedding in Paris,
                She's going to be married,
                And over a threshold she's going to be carried,
                The happiest bride you will see,
                Ah, *oui!*   You'll see.
                A wedding in Paris there'll be,
                Ah, *oui, oui, oui!*
                A wedding in Paris there'll be,
                Ah, *oui, oui, oui!*
ALICE [*spoken; frantically*]   Angy, child!
                              ANGY, *waving, runs off up* L *above the house.*   ALICE *weeps.*

CHORUS.   A wedding in Paris there'll be.
                              The CHORUS *turn and wave.   The train whistle off sounds alarmingly close.*
                              The lights dim to BLACK-OUT *as*—
                                                                                    LIGHTING CUE 1
                              the RUNNING TABS *close*
                              The lights come up.
                                                                                    LIGHTING CUE 2
                              The music continues, spiritedly.   ANGY *crosses hurriedly in front of the* RUNNING TABS *from* L *to* R, *holding her hat with one hand and clutching her bag with the other.   The* CROWD *follows, shouting " Good-bye, Angy ", " Be good ", " Come back, Angy ", " Don't talk to strangers ".   All are running fast, crossing from* L *to exit* R.   CHURCHILL *is the last to cross, shouting " Wait for me ".   The train whistle dissolves in the sound of a ship's siren.   The music continues.*

                                           SCENE 2
                              The Ship's rail, S.S. " Queen Anne "

The setting is a vignette of the alleyway between a front-cloth depicting the exterior of the deck cabins, and the ship's rail.   When looking over the rail towards the audience, the players are presumed to be looking down at the quay side.   A small trunk and a small bale are on the deck against the cabin walls.

WEDDING IN PARIS ACT I

When the RUNNING TABS *open, the ship's siren is sounding for sailing time. Merry farewells, laughter and voices are heard off.* PAUL CHANDLER *is standing* R, *looking over the rail. He is young, debonair, and self-confident with a relaxed air and humorous smile. Like most young men of his profession he likes to think of himself as cynical, and will say hard-boiled things so that no-one will think him soft or sentimental. The* CHIEF STEWARD *enters* R.

MUSIC

CHIEF STEWARD. This way, Madame Thibault. [*He crosses to* LC]

          MARCELLE THIBAULT *enters* R, *crosses to* C *and looks over the rail. The music fades. There is another blast from the ship's siren.*

Nice to have you on the ship again, Madame Thibault. Where would you like your deck-chair ? On the sunny side ?
 MARCELLE. On the wealthy side.
 PAUL. That lets me out.
            MARCELLE *turns and looks at Paul. The* CHIEF STEWARD *exits* L.
 MARCELLE. What a pity I didn't say on the charming side.
 PAUL. Save those extravagant words for a millionaire.
 MARCELLE. I always speak honestly to newspaper reporters, Mr Chandler.
 PAUL [*moving to* R *of Marcelle*] So you remember me ?
 MARCELLE. Naturally. [*She shakes hands with Paul*] At my last divorce you nice young reporters were my only consolation.
 PAUL. What about the fifty million pesetas ?
 MARCELLE. The peseta has been devalued.
 PAUL. Going back to Paris, I suppose ? Are you marrying any rich men this season ?
 MARCELLE [*moving close to him*] Are you speaking as a reporter or a fellow-traveller ?
 PAUL. I'm afraid I can't afford to be your fellow-traveller, Madame Thibault.
 MARCELLE [*moving to* C *of the rail*] Now, please, do you really think I am so mercenary ? It's my little tragedy that I cannot help falling for millionaires.
 PAUL. You make me weep.
 MARCELLE. They make *me* weep. They're always so disappointing. Oh, for some real romance in my life.
 PAUL. But what's more romantic to the public than a front-page divorce ?
 MARCELLE. There's another of my little tragedies, that my broken heart should provide amusement for the reading public.
 PAUL. Still, I bet you could get ten grand for writing a Sunday feature about your love life.
 MARCELLE. Thank you, I bet I could get twenty grand from any of my husbands for not writing it.
 PAUL. What a dame ! And you say you are not mercenary.
 MARCELLE [*leaning on the rail*] There are better ways of making a living than writing for the Sunday papers.
 PAUL. What have you got against the Press ?
 MARCELLE. You can never trust the newspapers.

         "IT'S NEWS"   No. 5

         MARCELLE *and* PAUL

MARCELLE.   I'm a victim of the gapers,
       Who have read about my capers,
       Seen my picture in the papers ev'ry day.
       Even yokels with bifocals
       Read about me in their locals,
       And they know most everything I do and say.
       There are rumours always rife,
       Of my very very public private life.

       If I fall in love, it's news,
       If I drop a glove, it's news,

BOTH.
    If I take a snooze,
    Or I get the blues,
    If I blow a fuse, it's news.
    If I woo a man, it's news,
    If I sue a man, it's news,
    If I've fed someone,
    If I wed someone,
    If I shed someone, it's news.
    Why, oh why, can't they leave me be?
    All I get's publicity!
    When I walk around, it's news,
    When I gain a pound, it's news,
    If I take a cruise, if I air my views,
    If a man I chooze, if I win or lose,
    It's always, always, always, always,
    Always in the news.

The ship's siren sounds.

MARCELLE. I think we're about to sail; I must go down and see about my luggage. [*She turns to exit* L]

ANGY enters L *and bumps into* MARCELLE. *ANGY carries a small book.*

ANGY. Oh, I beg your pardon.
MARCELLE. That's quite all right.

MARCELLE exits L. *ANGY stares after her. She moves* C, *glances at Paul and would like to ask about the dazzling Marcelle, but she is too shy to speak to a strange man. The siren sounds.* ANGY *puts her book on the rail and looks out front.*

PAUL. Well, we're off.

ANGY bursts into tears.

What's the matter?
ANGY. It's so wonderful.
PAUL. What?
ANGY. Everything.
PAUL. This tub?
ANGY. Just pure glamour.
PAUL. It's a good boat, but nothing to burst into tears about.

MRS PILCHARD, a great volcano of a woman, spouting authority, enters R *and crosses to* L *of Angy.*

ANGY [*to Paul*] I guess I ought to be more blasé in First Class, but I've never been on an ocean liner before. I have never even seen an ocean.
MRS PILCHARD. Wait till you've crossed as many times as I have. [*She speaks across Angy to Paul*] Forty-seven times I've traversed this duck-pond with my girls and never a well moment.
ANGY. Your girls? How many children have you?
MRS PILCHARD [*giggling*] Ask him. He knows all about my little girls.
ANGY. Why? Is he the father?

MRS PILCHARD giggles inanely.

PAUL. Madame Pilchard is principal of a very successful dancing academy in New York and her dancers appear at all the best theatres and clubs in America and on the Continent. When her dancers appear in Paris I usually " cover " them for my newspaper—and believe me they need some covering at times.
MRS PILCHARD. Yes, we are on our way to appear at the *Café des Étoiles*—but the *pièce de résistance* —whatever that may mean—is that my dancers have been honoured to appear in a command performance at a garden party before the President of France and his wife.

ANGY. How wonderful!
PAUL. Congratulations. That will be quite a scoop for my paper.
MRS PILCHARD. You know, I call my dancers my little sardines. Madame Pilchard's little sardines.
[*She laughs alone at her silly joke and nearly loses her hat overboard as she slaps the rail. She quickly recovers*] Good heavens! Water! The Atlantic. Meanest ocean in the business.
ANGY. Do you think it'll be rough?
MRS PILCHARD. No matter what people tell you, dear, this is the worst season.
ANGY. I'm not worried. Nothing ever makes me ill.
MRS PILCHARD. Ah! At sea it's the healthy who suffer most. How do you feel now?
ANGY. Great.
MRS PILCHARD. Oh, don't try to be brave, dear. It's always easier when you give in to that queasy feeling.
ANGY. Is it? [*She considers a moment*] How does that queasy feeling feel?
MRS PILCHARD. Terrible. [*She grimaces and sways backward and forward*] You must feel it a bit.
ANGY [*feeling uneasy*] A little bit.
MRS PILCHARD. Oh, you poor girl, and we're only in the harbour. Wait till we get out to sea.
ANGY [*worried*] Will it be worse?
MRS PILCHARD [*ominously shaking her head*] Come with me, dear, and I'll give you a lovely pill.
ANGY. Not till I've seen the Statue of Liberty.
MRS PILCHARD [*after a pause*] I'm afraid you're in for a very rough crossing, dear.

MRS PILCHARD *exits* L.

[*As she goes; calling*] Steward!
ANGY [*turning to Paul*] Oh, dear, I'd better be getting down to my cabin. [*She looks slightly alarmed and moves* L, *leaving her book on the rail*]
PAUL. Just a moment. [*He picks up the book*] Isn't this yours?
ANGY. Oh, yes, it is. Thank you so very much. [*She moves to* L *of Paul and holds out her hand for the book*]

PAUL *retains the book and looks at the title.*

PAUL. Going to France, I see.
ANGY [*as though she were going to heaven*] To Paris!
PAUL. First time?
ANGY. It's my first trip anywhere. Have you ever been to Paris?
PAUL. I live there.
ANGY. Imagine me meeting someone who *lives* in Paris. You must speak French.
PAUL. It's necessary.
ANGY. Is it really?
PAUL. Don't worry. They speak English at all the hotels. And if they don't, I'll be there to help you out.
ANGY. I'll have all the help I need, thank you.
PAUL. Have you friends in Paris?
ANGY. My fiancé speaks perfect French.
PAUL [*edging off*] You're engaged?
ANGY [*holding out her hand to display her ring*] I'm going to be married in Paris.
PAUL [*recovering his composure*] Oh, I hope you'll be happy.
ANGY. Thank you.
PAUL [*turning away*] Pleasant crossing.
ANGY. The same to you.

PAUL *turns to exit* R *and* ANGY *turns to exit* L. *They both stop and look back at each other.*

Is it true that you are a newspaper reporter?
PAUL [*taking a card from his pocket*] In case you need any help some day when your fiancé isn't around—[*he hands her the card*] take this.
ANGY [*reading the card*] "Paul Chandler—Dominions Press Limited." I've always dreamed of meeting a foreign correspondent.

Scene 2   WEDDING IN PARIS

PAUL. Just an ordinary reporter.   MUSIC
ANGY. Oh, imagine knowing someone who meets ambassadors and movie stars and murderers and Peers of the realm. Do you go to those big international weddings?
PAUL [*becoming amused by her earnestness*] And all the big international funerals, too.
ANGY. I'd perish of rapture.
PAUL [*laughing*] You perish often, don't you?
ANGY. I believe in living dangerously.
                            PAUL *laughs.*
Well, it was nice meeting you. [*She shakes hands with Paul*] Good-bye. [*She turns to go*]
PAUL. Good-bye—Miss Dobson.
ANGY [*turning*] How do you know my name?
PAUL. I read it in a book. [*He opens the book and reads the flyleaf*] " If this book should chance to roam, box its ears and send it home—to Angela Emily Dobson."
ANGY. Give it to me, please.
PAUL [*reading the title*] " French in Ten Words a Day."

LIGHTING CUE 3

" THE FRENCH LESSON "   No. 6

ANGY and PAUL

PAUL, *teasing, keeps the book from Angy as he sings.*

PAUL.	Pardon me, please, I'd like to ask you, If you have learned ten words today?
ANGY.	My thirst for French, as was expected, Has been neglected this busy day.
PAUL.	You can learn more by conversation And learn to speak with perfect ease. I'll take in hand your education, Now, I'm the teacher, attention, please. When I say, " *Embrassez moi* ", You say, " *Oui* ".
ANGY.	*Oui?*
PAUL.	When I ask you, *deux, trois fois,* You say, " *Oui* ".
ANGY [*obediently*]	*Oui.*
PAUL.	Say, if someone else should ask, " *Non, merci* ". Then when I say, " *Je vous aime* ", Oh, *cherie,* Say, when I say, " *Je vous aime* " " *Moi aussi* ".
ANGY.	I've never been much of a scholar, I only learned to sew and cook.
PAUL.	I'd like to bet my bottom dollar, That I could teach you more than a book.
ANGY.	You've been so kind and very patient, Where my enlightenment's concerned, [*She takes the book from him*] Now I'll repeat to you, dear teacher, All you have taught me, all I have learned. [*She opens the book*] When you say, " *Embrassez moi* ", I say,
PAUL.	" *Oui* ".

ANGY.   *Non!*
                   When you ask me *deux, trois fois*
PAUL [*pleading*] You say " *Oui* ".
ANGY.   *Non!*
PAUL [*trying to embrace her*]
                   Let me demonstrate to you.
ANGY.   *Non, merci.*
                   Then when you say, " *Je vous aime* ",
                   Oh, *cherie,*
PAUL [*expectantly*] Then when I say, " *Je vous aime* ",
ANGY.   I'll say, " *Bonne Nuit!* "

ANGY *snaps her book shut and exits* L. *The lights* BLACK-OUT *as—*

LIGHTING CUE 4

the RUNNING TABS *close*

The PASSENGERS *enter in front of the* RUNNING TABS. *The lights come up.*

LIGHTING CUE 5

" IN A COSY CORNER OF THE UPPER DECK "

No. 6a

CHORUS

We play games many games on the ocean,
There is shuffleboard and tennis on the deck,
But the best game of all is played by moonlight
In a cosy corner on the upper deck.
We may dance all the night till the dawning
And our beauty sleep it always seems to wreck,
But the best games of all are played by moonlight
In a cosy corner on the upper deck.
It's romantic on the sea, so romantic on the sea
Many many hearts are lost at sea.
You will vow never-ending devotion,
Your emotion you can never seem to check
Till the next time you fall in love by moonlight
In a cosy corner on the upper deck.

The Refrain is repeated.

LIGHTING CUE 6

The RUNNING TABS *open*

SCENE 3

The sun terrace, S.S. " Queen Anne "

It is an uncovered section of the promenade deck, equipped for deck sports, sunning, lounging and drinking. There are deck-chairs, lounge chairs, tables and sunshades. The entrance to the bar is R.

When the RUNNING TABS *open, some of the* PASSENGERS *move up stage and sit on the chairs, drinking. Other* PASSENGERS, *the girl dancers, lie on the deck, sun bathing.*

SHIP BALLET

No. 7

The MALE DANCERS *enter. The* GIRL DANCERS *rise and all join in the Ballet which takes the form of deck games, physical exercises, etc. At the end of the Ballet the* DANCERS *and other* PASSENGERS *exit.*

JACQUES DEVALLÉE *enters from the bar* R. *He is in his forties, distinguished and with the self-confidence of a man who always*

SCENE 3   WEDDING IN PARIS

gets his own way. When he is amused he can be boyish and buoyant, but when he is disinterested, his indifference is icy. He carries a newspaper. He sits in the lounge chair RC, *lights a cigarette and reads his paper.*

MRS PILCHARD *enters down* L *and stands* LC.

MRS PILCHARD [*calling*] Steward!

The 2ND STEWARD *enters* L, *quickly moves a chair from* L *and sets it behind* MRS PILCHARD, *who sits.*

The CHIEF STEWARD *enters from the bar* R *and crosses to Mrs Pilchard. He carries a tray and napkin.*

CHIEF STEWARD. Yes, Madam?
MRS PILCHARD. A brandy and soda.
CHIEF STEWARD. Brandy, madam?
MRS PILCHARD. You heard. After forty-seven crossings . . .
CHIEF STEWARD [*with resignation*] Yes, madam, brandy and soda. [*He nods to the 2nd Steward*]

The 2ND STEWARD *crosses and exits to the bar. The* CHIEF STEWARD *moves to the table up* R *and puts the dirty glasses on his tray.*

ANGY *enters from the bar* R, *moves down* R *and crosses to* L. *Aware of her loneliness she is highly self-conscious, and pretends to be looking for someone.* JACQUES *looks up and notices her as she crosses below him.*

ANGY [*to Mrs Pilchard*] Good morning.
MRS PILCHARD. Why, hello, dear.
ANGY. Isn't it a lovely day?
MRS PILCHARD. Would be if it weren't for this wicked sea.
ANGY. But it's quieter than a bowl of soup.

During the ensuing dialogue, the 2ND STEWARD *enters from the bar. He carries a tray with a brandy and soda and a chit pad and pencil. He crosses to* MRS PILCHARD *who signs the pad and takes the drink. The* CHIEF STEWARD *moves to the table down* R *and collects the glasses on to his tray.* JACQUES *beckons to the* CHIEF STEWARD *who moves to* R *of him, leaving his tray on the table.*

MRS PILCHARD. Don't mention soup.
ANGY. Personally, I'm disappointed in the ocean.
MRS PILCHARD. Come and have a drink with me.
ANGY. But I've just had breakfast.

JACQUES *whispers to the* CHIEF STEWARD *who takes a passenger list from his pocket, gives it to Jacques and points out Angy's name. The* 2ND STEWARD *crosses up* R.

MRS PILCHARD. On board one should never take anything solid before eleven.
ANGY. I feel fine.
MRS PILCHARD. That's what you said yesterday, and where were you last night?

JACQUES *whispers again to the* CHIEF STEWARD *who beckons to the* 2ND STEWARD *and gives him some instructions.*

The 2ND STEWARD *exits to the bar* R.

ANGY. In my cabin.
MRS PILCHARD. You see!
ANGY. There was nothing wrong with me except a weak character. The dining-room was so full of faces and—suppose I'd been seasick or made a *faux pas* the first night. I loathe cowardice.
MRS PILCHARD. A brandy and soda. That'll put you back on your feet. [*She drains her glass*]
ANGY. I'm on them now.
MRS PILCHARD. Take my advice. [*She rises*] Forty-seven crossings and the only thing that's kept me on my feet. [*She moves towards Angy, but stops and totters back to her chair*] Steward.

CHIEF STEWARD [*crossing quickly to Mrs Pilchard*] Yes, madam?   MUSIC
MRS PILCHARD [*handing him her glass*] Another brandy and soda.
CHIEF STEWARD [*fanning her with his napkin*] Yes, madam. [*He turns to Angy*] Miss Dobson?
ANGY. Yes, that's me.
CHIEF STEWARD. Monsieur Devallée's compliments and he would like to know if you'll take a glass of champagne with him.
ANGY. Champagne?
MRS PILCHARD. Champagne, you couldn't make a worse *faux pas*. [*She rises and takes Angy's arm*] Better let me take care of you, dear. I guarantee an uneventful crossing.

> *The 2ND STEWARD enters from the bar. He carries a tray with a bottle of champagne in a cooler and two champagne glasses. He puts the tray on the small table* RC, *then exits to the bar.*

ANGY [*withdrawing her arm*] I'm sorry, but I really have to go over and talk to Mr—Mr . . .
CHIEF STEWARD. Monsieur Devallée.
ANGY. Monsieur Devallée. He's an old friend of my family.
MRS PILCHARD. If you take my advice . . . [*She staggers a little*]
CHIEF STEWARD [*assisting Mrs Pilchard*] Allow me, madam.
MRS PILCHARD. Oh, if it would only stop rolling . . .

> MRS PILCHARD, *assisted for a few steps by the* CHIEF STEWARD, *staggers off* L. ANGY *looks around for Jacques. The* CHIEF STEWARD *indicates Jacques, then crosses to the lounge chair up* R *and sets it* L *of the table* RC. ANGY *crosses to* RC.

JACQUES [*rising*] How do you do?
ANGY. Oh!
JACQUES. I am the old friend of your family.
ANGY. How do you do?
JACQUES. I'm delighted to meet you, Miss Dobson. How is everyone in Hitchemup?
ANGY. How do you know where I come from?

> *The* CHIEF STEWARD *opens the champagne and fills the glasses.*

JACQUES. No one will put on a passenger list that one is from Hitchemup, Saskatchewan, unless one was from Hitchemup, Saskatchewan.
ANGY. Have they put my name in print?
JACQUES. Yes, of course. Would you like to see it?
ANGY. Please.
JACQUES [*looking through the passenger list*] Here we are, A—B—C—D—ah, Dobson. [*He shows Angy the entry*]
ANGY [*reading*] "Miss A. Dobson, Hitchemup, Saskatchewan." I feel quite famous.
JACQUES. Please sit down and let us drink to your new-found fame. [*He hands the passenger list to the Chief Steward*] Thank you.

> ANGY *sits* L *of the table.* JACQUES *sits* R *of it and hands a glass of champagne to her.*
>
> *The* CHIEF STEWARD *collects his tray of glasses and exits to the bar.*

ANGY [*looking anxiously at her drink*] Is this real champagne? In the morning?
JACQUES. Cordon Rouge 'forty-seven.
ANGY. How you say that! Just like the movies. I've never had champagne before. Suppose it did something funny to me?
JACQUES. I would never offer wine to a young lady that does something funny to her—permanently.

> PAUL *enters from the bar and pauses a moment above the table.*

[*To Paul. Without looking up*] No, thank you, one bottle is enough. [*He looks up and sees Paul*] Oh, I beg your pardon.

> PAUL *crosses and exits* L.

ANGY. I suppose I should try it. Just for the experience.

SCENE 3   WEDDING IN PARIS

> JACQUES *raises his glass.* ANGY *imitates him. They smile and drink.* ANGY *grimaces.*   MUSIC

JACQUES. Don't you like it?
ANGY. Hasn't it gone sour?
JACQUES. Perhaps you would prefer an ice-cream?
ANGY. Oh, no. I'll have to cultivate an expensive taste. [*She drinks*] Who are you? Someone important?
JACQUES. Not very. President of a company called International Grain and . . .
ANGY [*interrupting*] Not International Grain and Cereal? *You* must know Dix.
JACQUES. What is Dix?
ANGY. Dixwood Aiken. He's got a tremendous position in the Paris office.
JACQUES [*pondering over the name*] We keep a large staff in the central bureau.
ANGY. If you don't know Dixwood Aiken, you can't possibly be connected with International Grain and Cereal.
JACQUES. Perhaps not. Perhaps I am an impostor.
ANGY [*laughing*] I like you anyway. I like champagne, too. I'm having a lovely time. I've always admired older men. [*She drinks*]

> JACQUES *winces slightly.*

JACQUES. How old do you think I am?
ANGY. Thirty-five at least.
JACQUES. Oh, I'm much older. I'm already thirty-seven.
ANGY. You're well-preserved.
JACQUES. Thank you.
ANGY [*as an afterthought*] Are you married?
JACQUES [*laughing*] Suppose I were?
ANGY [*putting her glass on the table*] I cannot accept any more of your champagne until you have answered my question.

> JACQUES *picks up* ANGY's *glass and gently gives it to her.*

JACQUES. You can drink my wine with a clear conscience.

> PAUL *enters up* L, *crosses and exits* R.

Hullo, there he is again—poor young man, he does look offended. [*He raises his glass*] Drink! It's good champagne.

> *They drink.*

ANGY. Is it very expensive?
JACQUES. Thousands and thousands of French francs.
ANGY. Excuse me for asking.
JACQUES. Why?
ANGY. Where I come from it's considered bad form to talk about money.
JACQUES. And good form to talk about love?
ANGY. Of course.
JACQUES. In France we are more realistic. We speak frankly about money so that we can spend our wit and eloquence on the illusions of life—taste and art, beauty, love.

> MARCELLE *enters from the bar* R *and looks around. The* CHIEF STEWARD *follows her on. He carries Marcelle's handy-bag and magazine.*

ANGY. Illusions?
JACQUES. What else?

> MARCELLE *watches Angy and Jacques for a few moments.*

ANGY. I have never in my life heard anything so—so pagan.
JACQUES. Would you consider it more civilised to treat love as a substance and money as a dream?

> MARCELLE, *unseen by* JACQUES, *moves to the chair* R *of him and sits.* MUSIC
> *The* CHIEF STEWARD *gives Marcelle her magazine and bag, sees she is comfortable and exits to the bar.*

ANGY. Do you know what I think about you?
JACQUES. Do tell me.
ANGY. I think you have been disappointed in love.
JACQUES. I am sorry to disillusion you.
ANGY. Only a person who has been deeply hurt could be so cynical.

> JACQUES *sits up. As he does so, his elbow touches Marcelle and he realizes someone is there.*

JACQUES [*turning*] I beg your . . . Marcelle!
MARCELLE. Jacques, you old darling!

> JACQUES *and* MARCELLE *embrace lustily.*

JACQUES. I had no idea you were on this ship.
MARCELLE. And our chairs side by side. What a coincidence! It's been ages since we met. St Moritz, wasn't it? Or Chamonix. Who was I married to?
JACQUES. The Greek in oil, wasn't it?

> *The* CHIEF STEWARD *enters from the bar. He carries a champagne glass on his tray. He puts the glass on the table beside Jacques, then exits to the bar.*

MARCELLE. Oh, no, he could hardly walk, let alone ski. No, it must have been Deauville and the Maharajah. No—Eden Roc and my second earl—oh, well—very little difference.
JACQUES. May I introduce Miss Dobson? Madame . . . What is your name this season?
MARCELLE. Just as it was, Jacques, when we first met. Marcelle Thibault.
ANGY. Marcelle Thibault, the international ex-wife! Oh—I've read all about you in the Sunday papers.
MARCELLE. I do hope you've enjoyed it. Jacques darling, you are handsomer and younger than ever—you don't look a day over forty.

> PAUL *enters down* R, *crosses and exits down* L. JACQUES *watches him cross, then pours a glass of champagne for Marcelle and hands it to her.*

JACQUES [*to Angy*] Now who is that energetic young man? Is he also an old friend of the family?
ANGY. He's a very important foreign correspondent with a big job in Paris.
JACQUES. Foreign correspondent. [*To Marcelle*] Then he has promised to show her the city as no Parisian ever could.
ANGY. There's no reason for you to be snobbish. I'll probably never see him again after the ship lands.
JACQUES. Don't you like him?
ANGY. I won't see you, either, so please don't get any ideas. After I get off this boat it will be impossible for me to see any more men.
JACQUES. Are you entering a convent?

> PAUL *enters up* L, *crosses and sits at the table* R, *and looks directly at Angy.*

ANGY. I'm going to be married.
MARCELLE. How splendid!
JACQUES. Let us drink to the occasion.

> *They raise their glasses.*

MARCELLE. To a happy first marriage.
ANGY. To Dixwood Aiken.
JACQUES. And to five days on the boat.

> *They drink.* ANGY, *flustered by Paul's direct glance, puts her glass down and rises.*

SCENE 3 WEDDING IN PARIS

MUSIC

ANGY. Well, I think I'd better be getting down to my cabin.
JACQUES [*putting his glass down*] If your head's fuzzy, I know of a better way to clear it. [*He rises and offers his arm to Angy*]
ANGY. Oh, do you? [*She takes Jacques' arm*]

JACQUES *leads* ANGY *to Paul.* PAUL *rises.*

JACQUES. Young man, Miss Dobson would enjoy a walk around the deck before lunch.
PAUL. Thanks, chum. I'll do the same for you some time. [*To Angy*] Come on. [*He takes her arm*]

ANGY *and* PAUL *cross and exit up* L. MARCELLE *rises, puts her glass on the table and crosses to* C.

JACQUES [*crossing to* R *of Marcelle*] Refreshing, isn't she?
MARCELLE. Like Coca-Cola.
JACQUES. I've never tasted the stuff.
MARCELLE. No? It's not uninteresting at first. Bubbling and sweet but without stimulation.
JACQUES. I've never had a desire for unfermented drinks, but I might be tempted.
MARCELLE. At your age, it might prove indigestible.
JACQUES. Marcelle, do I strike you as a man who's been disappointed in love?
MARCELLE. Exactly.
JACQUES. I do?

MARCELLE *takes* JACQUES' *arm and leads him up* C.

MARCELLE. Any grown man who hasn't been disappointed in love is either a corpse or an idiot. Everyone knows what a shock it was for you when that Contessa of yours eloped with a Brazilian.

They turn.

And in a private plane, too.

They walk down C.

JACQUES. I lent it to them.
MARCELLE. You're too kind-hearted.
JACQUES. It's one of my disabilities. I even promoted him to manager of our South American branch.
MARCELLE. Didn't something of the same sort happen before? That long-legged English girl with the oversize tiara.
JACQUES. Ah! Yes, but she carried it magnificently.

They walk up C.

MARCELLE. Isn't she also married to one of your business associates?

They walk down C.

JACQUES. The happiest couple in Calcutta. They've named their son after me.
MARCELLE. How nice! Are all your old flames cosily married in distant outposts of your far-flung Empire?
JACQUES. I hope so.
MARCELLE. It must cost the office a lot of money.
JACQUES. No. It all comes off the Income Tax. [*He moves to the table* RC] Have another glass of champagne.
MARCELLE. No, thank you. [*She moves to* L *of Jacques*] I have a date with the hairdresser. Shall we lunch together?
JACQUES. I'm afraid I'm engaged.
MARCELLE. Oh! [*She crosses below Jacques and stands down* RC] How old do you think she is?
JACQUES [*moving to* L *of Marcelle*] Who?
MARCELLE [*turning to him*] Miss Coca-Cola, the pause that refreshes.
JACQUES. Oh—about eighteen.
MARCELLE. Fancy! And you?

MARCELLE *laughs and exits down* R.

LIGHTING CUE 7

		MUSIC
	"THE YOUNG IN HEART"	No. 8

JACQUES *and* CHORUS

JACQUES. The young in heart are always young,
Be young in heart, and you'll be young.
The winter comes when birds take wing,
But if there's sunshine in your heart
It's always Spring.
Though Autumn leaves must fall some day,
Love treats September just like May,
Time doesn't matter when you hear a love song sung,
The young in heart are always young.

You feel as young as you are,
You are as young as you feel,
There is no past and no future,
Only the present is real.
Some may grow old in their prime,
Some may stay young all the time,
'Cause they believe in the truth
Of the fountain of youth.

The young in heart are always young,
Be young in heart and you'll be young.
The Winter comes when birds take wing,
But if there's sunshine in your heart
It's always Spring.
Though Autumn leaves must fall some day,
Love treats September just like May.
Time doesn't matter when you hear a love song sung,
The young in heart are always young.

The music continues. The lights BLACK-OUT *as—*

LIGHTING CUE 8

the RUNNING TABS *close*

LIGHTING CUE 9

The lights come up.
The PASSENGERS *enter* R *and* L *in front of the* RUNNING TABS.

CHORUS. The young in heart are always young,
Be young in heart and you'll be young.
The Winter comes when birds take wing,
But if there's sunshine in your heart
It's always Spring, it's always Spring.
Though Autumn leaves must fall some day,
Love treats September just like May.
Time doesn't matter when you hear a love song sung,
The young in heart are always young.

SOLO VOICE. The young in heart are always young,
Be young in heart and you'll be young.
The winter comes when birds take wing,
But if there's sunshine in your heart
It's always Spring.

Scene 4	WEDDING IN PARIS	

CHORUS. Though Autumn leaves must fall some day,
Love treats September just like May.
Time doesn't matter when you hear a love song sung,
The young in heart are always young.
The young in heart are always young.

The lights BLACK-OUT

LIGHTING CUE 10

The PASSENGERS *exit* R *and* L

Scene 4

The ship's rail, S.S. "Queen Anne"

FAIRY TALE AND "LOVELY LADY OF THE SANDS"

No. 9

JACQUES

When the RUNNING TABS *open, it is night.* ANGY *and* JACQUES, *dressed in evening clothes, are in earnest conversation.* ANGY *is* L *of Jacques. The music accompanies softly throughout.*

ANGY. Five perfect days and I've loved every minute. And wasn't it kind of the moon to be full on our last night?
JACQUES. Are you sorry it's our last night?
ANGY. If I wasn't enjoying myself so much I'd be having a wonderful time.
JACQUES. Your logic eludes me.
ANGY. You're a fascinating man of the world and—[*She lifts her left hand and looks at her ring*] I'm engaged to be married.
JACQUES [*pushing her hand down; with a slight groan*] Must you always talk about it?
ANGY. You're always forgetting.
JACQUES. In my whole life I've never encountered a woman so faithful.
ANGY. Then you've never been loved.
JACQUES. Perhaps. You see, I have been admired, flattered, diverted, pursued . . .
ANGY. But never loved?
JACQUES. My own fault. At the first sight of sincerity I run away. Perhaps I was afraid of being disappointed again.
ANGY [*gleefully*] What did I tell you?
JACQUES. Would you like to hear the story of my disappointment?
ANGY. Oh, please.
JACQUES. I have never told it to another woman.
ANGY. I'll never betray you. Is it very sad?
JACQUES. Oh—tragic! Once I fell in love with a sea nymph.
ANGY. But I thought it was a true story.
JACQUES. A sea nymph in a white bathing costume.
ANGY. Oh, a girl!
JACQUES. Her hair had the golden lustre of summer sand and her little hands—[*with a rapturous sigh*] her little hands were seashells. On warm afternoons she lay curled under a parasol whose colour gave a touch of green to her foam-white skin.
ANGY. You *were* in love.
JACQUES. I was! For hours on end I watched her from a hiding place among the rocks, holding my breath for ecstasy. It's a miracle I did not choke to death holding my breath for so long.
ANGY. Didn't you ever speak to her?
JACQUES. No. She was always surrounded by Vikings, great enormous fellows, all bronze and broad —and enormous . . .
ANGY. Just like Dix!
JACQUES. Yes, but at night—at night I had her for my own. She'd come to the beach to play, to float and frolic in the water until a monster wave attacked her. Then I leaped from the highest rock, and . . .
ANGY. And?

JACQUES. We perished together.
ANGY. Oh, a dream.
JACQUES. But poignant. One morning I found her parasol on the shore, broken, water-soaked, its green silk shredded like seaweed. At once I took the next bus—travelled to the nearest town where I found another parasol—green. It cost one pound, eight shillings and ninepence, which left me penniless. So I was obliged to walk back, trudging through hot sunshine while I composed a poem.
ANGY. Go on.
JACQUES. I found her on the beach surrounded by her Vikings. No longer shy I bounded into their midst. With my poem on my lips I laid my gift at her feet. She laughed.
ANGY. With joy?
JACQUES. With scorn. Because her favourite Viking had teased her for carrying a parasol and she had helped him destroy it. And now I came with another one to embarrass her.
ANGY. She ought've been grateful. Didn't she say anything?
JACQUES. Yes—" You've got a dirty face, you ugly little boy ".
ANGY. Ugly! But you must have been handsome when you were young.
JACQUES. All hands and ears. And boney as one is at thirteen.
ANGY. Thirteen—well, how old was she?
JACQUES. Oh, getting on—quite seventeen. How they laughed at my parasol and my poem.
ANGY [*moving close to Jacques and holding his hands*] Poor little Jacques. I shouldn't have laughed. How did the poem go?
JACQUES. It is very sentimental.
ANGY. Please.
JACQUES [*singing*] To my golden-haired Madonna,
Lovely lady of the sands,
Take this parasol I bring you
In your lily-white hands.
With my heart and my devotion,
May I offer you this prize?
'Tis the colour of the ocean
With the sheen of your eyes.
[*He puts his left arm slowly around Angy's shoulders*]
You hold my heart
In the palms of your hands,
Madonna mine,
Lovely lady of the sands.

At the end of the little song, JACQUES *and* ANGY *are very close together. They hold hands.*

JACQUES. How long is it since you've seen your fiancé?
ANGY. Sixteen months, three weeks and two days.
JACQUES. And in all that time you've never thought about another man?
ANGY [*pulling her hands away*] What kind of a girl do you think I am?

ANGY *exits* L. JACQUES, *watching her go, smiles to himself as the lights dim to* BLACK-OUT *and—*

LIGHTING CUE 11

the RUNNING TABS *close*

LIGHTING CUE 12

The PASSENGERS *enter in front of the* RUNNING TABS. *They wear evening dress and the* GIRLS *carry green parasols.*

REPRISE
" LOVELY LADY OF THE SANDS "
CHORUS

No. 9a

At the end of the number the PASSENGERS *exit* R *and* L. *The lights* BLACK-OUT.

LIGHTING CUE 13

SCENE 5

The sun terrace, S.S. "Queen Anne"

The terrace is dressed with fairy lights. There is a table R with three chairs, above, L and R of it, and there is a table L with two chairs R and L of it.

When the RUNNING TABS *open, it is a bright moonlit night and the fairy lights are lit. The* PASSENGERS *are grouped at the sides and back watching a Waltz Ballet performed by Mrs Pilchard's* DANCERS. PAUL *is seated* L *of the table* L, *glaring at a whisky and soda. A* LADY *and two* GENTLEMEN *are seated, drinking, at the table* R. *The* CHIEF STEWARD *is in attendance, standing in the bar doorway* R. MRS PILCHARD *is standing down* L.

WALTZ BALLET AND MELOS   No. 10

DANCERS

At the end of the Ballet the music is repeated. Two or three couples of the PASSENGERS *waltz quietly and gently at the back. The* DANCERS *and the remainder of the* PASSENGERS, *with the exception of the three at the table* R, *exit.*

MRS PILCHARD [*crossing to* R *of the table* L *; to Paul*] Well, Mr Chandler, what do you think of my little sardines?

PAUL. Enchanting, my dear Mrs Pilchard. They are very versatile. I rather felt you specialized in the Can-Can type of dance. [*He drains his glass*]

MRS PILCHARD. My dear Mr Chandler, with a dance floor likely to be rolling and pitching, I dare not risk such a dance. Far too dangerous. Why, with the flying splits one is likely to land on a boat-hook. By the way, I saw *your little partner* on the boat deck.

PAUL [*leaping up*] Alone?

MRS PILCHARD. She'd better watch her step. What those Frenchmen don't know about love hasn't been invented. [*She crosses to the table* R. *To one of the Men*] May I have the pleasure?

Paul resumes his seat and beckons to the Chief Steward.

MAN [*rising*] Wouldn't you rather have a highball?

MRS PILCHARD. After the waltz, Mr Seersucker.

MRS PILCHARD *determinedly waltzes the* MAN *out up* L, *loudly " la-la-ing " to the music. The* CHIEF STEWARD *crosses to Paul.*

PAUL [*to the Chief Steward*] Another, please.

CHIEF STEWARD [*collecting Paul's empty glass*] Double?

PAUL. Yeah.

The CHIEF STEWARD *crosses and exits* R.

MARCELLE *enters up* L *and moves down* LC.

[*He rises*] Marcelle, you look ravishing.

MARCELLE. Thanks, Paul.

PAUL. Come and have a drink with me. We can console each other.

MARCELLE *sits* R *of the table* L, PAUL L *of it.*

What'll it be?

MARCELLE. Chartreuse, small and green, but not for consolation. I am quite happy.

The CHIEF STEWARD *enters from the bar with Paul's drink, crosses and puts it on the table* L.

PAUL [*to the Chief Steward*] Small Green Chartreuse for Madame. [*He signs the chit for his drink*]

CHIEF STEWARD. Very good, sir.

The CHIEF STEWARD *crosses and exits* R.

PAUL. Happy, huh?

MARCELLE. Tomorrow I dine in Paris.

PAUL. There's a pensive look in your eyes. If I'm not wrong, you've been dreaming of Jacques' handsome income.

MARCELLE. You're quite wrong. One would never divorce Jacques Devallée.   MUSIC

The CHIEF STEWARD *enters from the bar with Marcelle's drink, crosses and puts it on the table* L.

CHIEF STEWARD. Chartreuse, madame.
MARCELLE. Oh, thank you. [*She drinks*]

PAUL *signs the chit for the drink. The* CHIEF STEWARD *crosses and stands by the bar doorway* R.

PAUL. Tell me something. Does that Casanova play fair with women?
MARCELLE. He is a gentleman.
PAUL [*rising and crossing to* C] He'd better act like one with *her* or he'll get his face pushed in.
MARCELLE. Why do you make a noise like a disappointed wolf? Angy is going to marry that young man in Paris.
PAUL [*turning to face Marcelle*] Which leaves you a clear field with Jacques.
MARCELLE [*bridling slightly*] I probably won't see him again until we meet by accident at some overcrowded resort.
PAUL. But you'd like to.
MARCELLE [*rising and moving to* L *of Paul*] You're quite wrong—Jacques and I have known each other since we bowled hoops together in the Bois.

The music ceases. The DANCING *couples exit.*

PAUL. Is that the best you could do with a boy in the Bois?

The GIRL *and* MAN *at the table* R *rise and exit to the bar* R.

MARCELLE [*crossing below Paul to* R *of him*] I had a Mamma.
PAUL. French girls always do.
MARCELLE. Mine happened to be English, but she believed in early marriages, marriages of convenience. [*She moves slowly* R]
PAUL. And lots of them.
MARCELLE. It *can* become a habit. [*She sits* L *of the table* R]
PAUL. And not a bad one, either. [*He crosses above the table* R *and sits* R *of it*] You must have had everything a girl ever dreams of.

" THE SIMPLE THINGS OF LIFE "   No. 11
MARCELLE

MARCELLE.
I've had my share of admiration,
I've been a poet's inspiration,
And yet I've missed so many things,
The things I've longed for,
The simple things of life.

I've been the centre of attraction,
And men have loved me to distraction
And yet I've missed the little things,
The things I've longed for,
The simple things of life.

To wander hand in hand just aimlessly
And never think of time,
To see a lot of happy kids at play
And wish that they were mine.
What good are diamonds when you're lonely?
I need someone to love me only,
And give me all those little things
I've always longed for,
The simple things of life.

SCENE 5 WEDDING IN PARIS

PAUL [*speaking over the music*] The simple things. They seem simple till you get them and then they turn into the same old complications. Life's too involved. MUSIC
MARCELLE. You're in love.
PAUL. So what!
MARCELLE. Take a chance, Paul. I know how lonely life can be.
PAUL. There are always people.
MARCELLE [*singing*] What good are people when you're lonely?
　　　　　　　　　　I need someone to love me only,
　　　　　　　　　　And give me all those little things
　　　　　　　　　　I've always longed for,
　　　　　　　　　　The simple things of life.

　　　　　　　　　　　　JACQUES *enters up* L *and crosses to the Chief Steward.*

JACQUES. Steward, have you seen Miss . . .?
MARCELLE. Come and join us, Jacques. On our last night we should have a little drink together.

　　　　　　　　　　　　MELOS　　　　　　　　　　　　　　No.11a

JACQUES [*over the music; reluctantly*] With pleasure—but I'm intruding.
MARCELLE. Not at all.
JACQUES [*to the Chief Steward*] Whisky.

　　　　　　　　　　　The CHIEF STEWARD *exits to the bar.*

PAUL [*rising and crossing below the table* C] I was just going, anyway, to look for Miss Dobson.
MARCELLE. Good luck, darling.
PAUL. Thanks.

　　　　　　　　　　　PAUL *exits up* L.

JACQUES [*moving above the table* R] You find him attractive?
MARCELLE. Sweet.
JACQUES. Such nice manners.
MARCELLE. Delightful.
JACQUES. What a pity he has no money. [*He moves the chair above the table to* R *of Marcelle and sits*] You'd make a charming pair.
MARCELLE. You're too kind.

　　　　　　　　　　　The CHIEF STEWARD *enters from the bar with Jacques' drink and puts it on the table* R.

JACQUES. He's obviously enchanted by you. [*He signs the chit for the drink*]

　　　　　　　　　　　The CHIEF STEWARD *exits to the bar.*

MARCELLE. Fiddlesticks!
JACQUES. But, Marcelle, at our age there is no tonic like youth.
MARCELLE. You haven't taken an overdose yourself by any chance?
JACQUES. Not yet. But the sea is so calm tonight, and the stars are so bright.
MARCELLE. And hasn't the moon gone to your head a little bit?
JACQUES. I just want everyone to be as happy as I am.
MARCELLE. Are you about to scatter rose petals?
JACQUES. Orchids for you, dear. Mauve ones. But seriously, Marcelle, why don't you take pity on the poor boy? Angy's far too young for him.
MARCELLE. For *him*?
JACQUES. She might do him permanent harm. The only way to become a man of the world is to be educated by a woman of the world, if you see what I mean.
MARCELLE. I'm beginning to!
JACQUES. And think how nice it would be for *you*. He could help to while away some lonely evenings in Paris.
MARCELLE. Where would you suggest I take him? The *Casino de Paris* or the *Folies Bergère*?

JACQUES. I wouldn't take him anywhere. Just light your prettiest candles with the pinkest shades and open a bottle of champagne, and if necessary add just a little brandy.
MARCELLE. How clever you are.
JACQUES. And don't forget my experience is always at your service.

PAUL *enters up* L *and sits dejectedly* R *of the table* L.

MARCELLE. Didn't you find her, Paul?
PAUL. Yeah. Watching the stars from the upper deck. She didn't feel like sharing them.

JACQUES *slips out of his chair, moves to the bar door* R, *turns, gives a mischievous glance at Marcelle and waves her over to Paul.* PAUL *looks up and sees Jacques waving.* JACQUES *waves to Paul and exits to the bar.*

I don't trust that guy.
MARCELLE [*laughing*] Neither do I. Paul—what would you say if I invited Angy to stay with me in Paris until her wedding?
PAUL. Why should you?
MARCELLE. I don't like to see a young girl unprotected.
PAUL. But she's going to be married right away.
MARCELLE. In France it takes ten days—and she ought to have some place where her friends can come to visit her.
PAUL [*rising and crossing to* C] Am I welcome?
MARCELLE [*rising and moving to* R *of Paul*] All her friends are welcome.
PAUL. Including Jacques?
MARCELLE [*with superb innocence*] Why not?
PAUL. Ten days. Huh! [*He crosses above Marcelle to* R *of her*] Madame, your technique's showing.
MARCELLE. A woman gets nowhere unless she uses intelligence. You must come to see Angy very often.
PAUL. It's a deal. [*He holds out his hand*] I'll take care of Angy. You handle Monsieur.
MARCELLE. It's a deal.

They shake hands.

PAUL. Want to dance?
MARCELLE. Thank you, Paul, but I feel I should go to my beauty sleep.
PAUL. A very wise suggestion—a nightcap for me then perchance to dream. *Au revoir.*

PAUL *exits to the bar. The music ceases.* MARCELLE *turns to exit up* L.

MRS PILCHARD [*off* L] No. [*Loudly*] No. Stop it, Mr Seersucker.

There is a sound off L *uncommonly like a slap on the face.*

MRS PILCHARD *enters down* L. *She is rather dishevelled.*

Men! They're all alike. [*She adjusts her hair, etc. and crosses to* L *of Marcelle*] I merely said to him, " May I have the pleasure? " I'm afraid his interpretation of the word " pleasure " didn't coincide with mine. Did you see my little dancers?
MARCELLE. Yes—I saw them from the upper deck. Delightful.
MRS PILCHARD. I am now working on a new ballet. I am calling it *The Spirit of France.*
MARCELLE. Is this the one to be performed before the President at the garden party which Paul has told me about?
MRS PILCHARD. Yes.
MARCELLE. I must congratulate you on such an honour.
MRS PILCHARD [*mincingly*] Thank you.
MARCELLE. When we get to Paris you are very welcome to use my grounds for rehearsals. What better inspiration could one get to devise a ballet entitled *The Spirit of France* than in the very gardens of the old Château de Foncelle where once Napoleon himself used to tread its paths.
MRS PILCHARD. Well, what d'you know! Madame Thibault—you are kindness itself. I will certainly take advantage of your offer.
MARCELLE. The château was burnt down—but the lovely grounds have always remained. I allow

Scene 5 WEDDING IN PARIS 23

tourists to visit the historic gardens once a week. They are always particularly interested in seeing a little old weather-beaten stone bench in one of the arbours. On it, it is said, Napoleon wooed Josephine.
Mrs Pilchard. On a stone bench! They certainly did things the hard way. Well, I must get to my cabin. [*She glances off* L] I wonder if that wolf has gone.
Marcelle. Come along. I will act as your bodyguard.

MUSIC

Marcelle *and* Mrs Pilchard *exit up* L.

MELOS   No. 11b

Paul *enters from the bar.*
Angy *enters up* R *and moves down* C. *Between* Paul *and* Angy *there is a certain constraint.*

Paul [*speaking over the music*] Would you like a drink? [*He crosses to* R *of Angy*]
Angy. Not particularly.
Paul. What about a walk on deck?
Angy. I'd rather stay here.
Paul. Want to dance?
Angy. No, thank you.
Paul. Well—if you don't like your music canned on the deck—would you care to go down to the ball-room?
Angy. No, thank you.
Paul [*with irritation*] Oh, climb off the high horse. You know you like to dance with me. [*He holds out his arms*]
Angy [*moving to him*] Only because you're a good dancer.

Paul *takes* Angy *in his arms and they dance.*

Paul [*as they dance*] Is your fiancé a good dancer?
Angy. He's a great football player. Not that I'm being disloyal. But facts are facts.
Paul. Angy, are you sure you want to marry the guy?

Angy *is silent for a split second, then stops dancing.*

Angy [*angrily*] Of course I'm sure. Naturally. Why else should I be going to Paris? You don't wait for a man six . . .

Paul *whirls her into a turn.*

Oh!
Paul [*mockingly*] Sixteen months, two weeks and three days.
Angy. Three weeks and two days. And I wish you wouldn't throw it up to me all the time. [*She pushes him away*]
Paul. Who's always throwing it up to me? You refuse to forget for five minutes . . .
Angy [*crossing to* R] I don't wish to discuss it again.
Paul [*crossing to* L] Neither do I.

They look at each other. Angy *looks quickly away.* Paul *crosses to her and tries to take her in his arms to resume the dance.*

Angy. No—I've got to go down to my cabin.

The music ceases.

Paul. Why do you have to go?
Angy. I don't want to stand around arguing with *you.*
Paul [*moving down* C] I don't like to argue with you, either. [*He turns*] Please stay.
Angy [*turning to him*] I really oughtn't.
Paul. Just for a moment.
Angy [*crossing slowly to him*] A moment can be something a person regrets for the rest of their lives.
Paul. Or remembers.

"IT ONLY TOOK A MOMENT"

ANGY and PAUL

PAUL.
It's funny when two people meet
And find themselves in love;
They blame it on the moonlight
Or the stars that shine above.
And tho' I don't believe in love at sight,
Our fate, it seems, will always guide us right.
[*He takes her hand*]

> *The* RUNNING TABS *close behind Paul and Angy, isolating them so that they are completely alone in their preoccupation with each other.*

It only took a moment to fall in love with you,
I saw you for a moment and then I knew.
There comes to perfect strangers
A spark we can't define,
I loved you from the moment your eyes met mine.
What happens now? Who can foresee?
Yet while you are here with me,
Let's live this precious moment
Before it disappears.
If we can take our fill of
The thrill of the moment,
Perhaps this precious moment
Will last for years.

The song continues.

SCENE 6

Another part of the ship's rail, S.S. "Queen Anne"

The scene is a front-cloth depicting the night sky beyond the ship's rail.
The RUNNING TABS *open behind Paul and Angy.*

ANGY.
I like the way you smile at me,
The way you hold me near,
And when we dance I like the things
You whisper in my ear.
But after all, we met but yesterday,
So why should I believe you when you say

It only took a moment to fall in love with you,
I saw you for a moment and then I knew.
There comes to perfect strangers
A spark one can't define,
I loved you from the moment your eyes met mine.
What happens now? Who can foresee?
Yet while you are here with me,
Let's live this precious moment
Before it disappears.
If we can take our

BOTH.
                fill of
The thrill of the moment,
Perhaps this precious moment
Will last for years.

SCENE 6   WEDDING IN PARIS

At the end of the song PAUL *takes* ANGY *in his arms. She tries conscientiously to draw back. He holds her closer; her protest grows weaker. Emboldened, he embraces her. She tries, dutifully, to resist, but the urge is too strong and she seizes the moment. With all her fervour, her youth, her excitement, she gives herself to the kiss. It is a climax. Both cling, then separate, then kiss again. As the second kiss grows intense,* ANGY *pulls away.* PAUL *tries to hold her tighter but she pushes away.*

MUSIC

ANGY. No, don't.

PAUL *again tries to kiss her.*

Please.
PAUL [*releasing her*] You're not still yearning for the Saskatchewan Romeo?
ANGY. Oh, let me alone.

PAUL *hesitates but sees Angy is sincere and exits* L. ANGY *starts to cry.* JACQUES *enters* R.

JACQUES [*crossing to Angy*] I've found you.
ANGY [*sobbing*] Go away, please.
JACQUES. You're crying.
ANGY. Oh, Jacques! [*She buries her head on his shoulder*]
JACQUES [*becoming very tender and putting his arm protectively around her*] Why? Tomorrow is the great day. We will be in France, and on the pier, waiting, you will find your fiancé.
ANGY. That's what I'm afraid of.
JACQUES. What did you say?
ANGY. I hate myself.
JACQUES. Why?
ANGY. He has been faithful and I—I—[*she falters, but manages to speak out*] I have fallen in love with another man.
JACQUES. Oh! Oh, my little one. [*He puts his arms around her*]

MELOS and CHOIR   No. 12a
CHORUS

ANGY. Since the first day on this ship it's been a losing struggle against temptation. Do you think I've got a weak character?
JACQUES. No, no, you're very strong, you're just honest with yourself. You'll be much happier for it.
ANGY. Oh, Jacques, what am I to do?
JACQUES [*tenderly*] Just go on being honest and leave the rest to me. [*His arm tightens around her*]
ANGY. Good night, Jacques, dear. [*She plants a girlish kiss on his cheek*]

JACQUES *takes his handkerchief from his breast pocket and gives it to* ANGY, *who wipes her eyes and returns it. Before tears can flow again,* ANGY *exits* L.

The CHORUS *are heard singing off.* JACQUES *smiles and replaces the handkerchief in his pocket.*

CHORUS.   Time doesn't matter when you hear a love song sung,
          The young in heart are always young.

The lights BLACK-OUT.

LIGHTING CUE 14

JACQUES *exits during the* BLACK-OUT.

The FRONT-CLOTH *rises*

The lights come up.

LIGHTING CUE 15

Scene 7

The Customs Shed, Le Havre

Streamers and banners to greet the arrival of a luxury liner make the Shed gay this sunny afternoon. Activity and excitement add to the vitality of the scene. Lamp-posts R and L are hung with handsome posters, showing the glories of Paris. Over the three low counters across the Shed hang letters A–B, C–D, E–F, etc. There are sections of barrier rails R and L.

HARBOUR BALLET

No. 13

Dancers and Chorus

When the Front-Cloth *rises, the* Male Dancers, *as* Customs Officers, *lounge on the benches. If there should be a shortage of male ballet dancers, girls could wear the uniform of the French Customs Officers. Their indolence and between-duty activities are a slow pantomic ballet which suddenly becomes lively as the music announces the arrival of the* Passengers *who burst in* R, *some carrying suitcases. They look around, some hurrying to the barriers* L, *and some to the footlights where they wave to their friends who are presumed to be waiting outside.* Porters, *carrying luggage, also enter* R. *A* Gendarme *stands at the barrier down* L.

Passengers.
We are here, we are here in the harbour,
In the harbour of Le Havre.
With excitement we're fraught,
For we've landed in port,
And we say "Hello" to France.
We are here all your friends and relations
From so many diff'rent nations.
Happy moments when we,
Standing here on the quay,
Want to say "Hello" to France.

Porters *and* Customs Officers.
And so we welcome all our visitors,
Our many friends and our inquisitors,
If you're from Tokio,
Or you're from Idaho,
We sing, we welcome you to France.

All.
We are here, we are here in the harbour,
In the harbour of Le Havre.
With excitement we're fraught,
For we've landed in port,
And we say "Hello" to France.
We are here all your friends and relations
From so many diff'rent nations.
Vive La France, we will cheer,
As we stand on the pier
And we say "Hello" to France.

During the remainder of the number, the Passengers, Porters *and the* Customs Officers *sing, and dance with the luggage etc. using the low counters. The* Customs Officers *examine the luggage, throwing the contents of the cases all over the place.*

All.
Customs, Customs,
Always Customs.
Go through Customs
Everywhere you go.
Turn your trunk out,
Drag your junk out,
You'll go through it
Everywhere you go.

SCENE 7	WEDDING IN PARIS	
PASSENGERS.	They just delay your getaway, And they love to make you pay.	MUSIC
ALL.	Customs, Customs, Go through Customs, Why we do it We will never know.	

We are here, we are here in the harbour,
In the harbour of Le Havre.
With excitement we're fraught,
For we've landed in port,
And we say " Hello " to France.
We are here all your friends and relations
From so many diff'rent nations.
Vive La France, we will cheer,
As we stand on the pier
And we say " Hello " to France.

The number ends with a picture. During the following dialogue, the PASSENGERS, PORTERS *and* CUSTOMS OFFICERS *deal quietly at the counters with the luggage, repacking and marking the cases.*

MRS PILCHARD *enters down* R, *and rushes across to the barrier down* L.

MRS PILCHARD [*to the Gendarme; imperiously*] Open this, please.
GENDARME. I regret, madame. Not before you have been through the Customs.
MRS PILCHARD. I've been through the Customs. Forty-seven times. Let me out.
GENDARME. Madame, it is the law.
MRS PILCHARD. You just try to get into the United States, you Communist. [*She shrugs and goes up* L]

MARCELLE *and* ANGY *enter down* R, *talking earnestly together.*

PAUL *follows them on, a few steps behind, but* ANGY *pretends not to be aware of him.*

ANGY [*as she enters*] No, Marcelle, thank you just the same. It's terribly generous, but I can't accept.

ANGY, MARCELLE *and* PAUL *cross to* C.

MARCELLE [L *of* ANGY] Listen, Angy, in France a respectable young girl does not stop alone at an hotel.
ANGY. After ten days I won't have to be respectable—I'll be married.
PAUL. In ten days a lot can happen.

JACQUES, *in high spirits, enters* R.

JACQUES [*crossing below Paul to* R *of* ANGY] Good morning.
ANGY. Good morning.
JACQUES [*exuberantly*] Angy, did you sleep well ? What a lovely day ! Have you ever seen brighter sunshine, a bluer sky, more sexy seagulls ? [*He crosses below Angy to* R *of Marcelle*] Good morning.

Two PORTERS *exit* R.

MARCELLE. Good morning. We have news for you. Angy is to stop with me at my house until she is married. Her friends can come and visit her whenever they like.
JACQUES. Have you still the same telephone number ?

The CHIEF STEWARD *enters* R. *He carries Jacques' overcoat and gloves.*

MARCELLE. I was sure you'd ask me that.
PAUL [*in an undertone*] So was I. [*He crosses above the others to* L *of Marcelle*]
CHIEF STEWARD [*moving* RC] Monsieur Devallée, you forgot your overcoat.
JACQUES. I've got it on. No, I haven't. [*He crosses to the Chief Steward*]
C

The CHIEF STEWARD *assists* JACQUES *to don his overcoat.* [MUSIC]

PAUL [*to Marcelle*]   Haven't you forgotten to give me your telephone number?
ANGY.   Will you please tell that person he will not be welcome. [*She turns away*]
MARCELLE [*to Paul*]   You heard what she said.
PAUL.   My hearing's not very good. What did she say?
MARCELLE.   That her friends may come to visit her whenever they like.

A PORTER *enters* R *with a trolley bearing Marcelle's luggage, crosses and wheels it up* L.

[*She sees her luggage*]   Oh, my luggage! How shall I explain my seven wedding rings? [*She follows the porter up* L]
PAUL [*to Angy*].   I'll look after your stuff, Angy.
ANGY.   Please don't bother. My fiancé will take care of everything. [*She rushes down* LC *and looks eagerly out over the audience*]

JACQUES *crosses to* R *of Angy.* PAUL *deliberates for a couple of seconds, then follows and stands* L *of Angy.*

[*She waves wildly to someone out front*]   Dix! Dix!   [*To Jacques*]   See him?
JACQUES.   Which one?
ANGY.   The handsome one with the broad shoulders.
JACQUES.   What beautiful padding. [*He crosses to the Chief Steward and collects his gloves*]
PAUL.   Does he look as good to you as he did sixteen months, three weeks and . . .
ANGY.   I believe I asked you never to speak to me again. This time I mean it. [*She looks off* L]   Look, there he is. [*She rushes to the Gendarme at the barrier* L]   Can't I get out, please?   Just for a minute.

JACQUES *crosses to Angy.*
The CHIEF STEWARD *exits* R.

I've got to speak to someone.
GENDARME.   Alas, Mademoiselle, sentiment must also comply with the law.
JACQUES.   Angy, I'll try to help you. I have a certain way with officials. [*He crosses to the Gendarme and gives him some franc notes*]   Ça va. Ça va. [*He turns to Angy*]   I'm trying to help you.
ANGY.   Oh, would you?   I just can't wait to meet Dix.
JACQUES.   Neither can I.

JACQUES *exits down* L.

A PORTER *enters* R *with Paul's and Angy's cases which he puts* C *of the downstage counter under the C–D section.* PAUL *moves and sits* C *on the downstage counter.* MRS PILCHARD *moves down* LC *to* R *of Angy.*

MRS PILCHARD.   You'd better go and look after your bags, dear. Why are mine always the last to come through? [*She crosses to* R *and calls*]   Steward!

MRS PILCHARD *rushes off* R. ANGY *looks around for the C–D section.*

PAUL.   Here's your place, Miss Dobson.
ANGY [*crossing to* RC]   I wish you'd stop following me around like a manhunt.
PAUL [*rising and moving to* L *of Angy*]   Sorry if my presence annoys you, but the law requires that the tourist await inspection under the initial letter of his surname.
ANGY.   The law doesn't require tourists to hold a conversation.
PAUL.   Why are you so afraid to talk to me?
ANGY.   Don't be so silly. What have I to be afraid of?
PAUL.   That you're deceiving yourself.
ANGY.   Not about Dix.
PAUL [*crossing to* LC]   No—about Angela Dobson who might be too loyal to a threadbare dream.
ANGY [*crossing to* R *of Paul*]   That's not true. And even if it were, I don't see how it could possibly concern you.
PAUL.   It might keep you from feeling the way you'd like to feel about me.
ANGY [*flaming*]   If you want to know how I feel about you, I—[*she splutters*] I—I . . .

SCENE 7 WEDDING IN PARIS

PAUL. Hate, loathe and despise me. [*He moves* L]
ANGY [*following Paul*] I do. I do.
    A CUSTOMS OFFICER *collects Angy's bag and moves to* R *of her with it.*
And this time I really mean it. [*She turns away to find the Customs Officer waiting*]
1ST CUSTOMS OFFICER. Bon jour, madame.
ANGY [*nervously*] Bon nuit. No. Merci—no—voilà—no . . . Qu'est-ce—que c'est . . . ?
PAUL. You've forgotten one. *Embrassez moi.*
ANGY. You keep out of this. [*She resolutely turns her back to him*]
PAUL. Just open your bags and close your mouth and everything will be all right.
    A 2ND CUSTOMS OFFICER *collects Paul's bag and crosses to* L *of Paul.*
1ST CUSTOMS OFFICER [*to Angy*] Anything to declare?

"I HAVE NOTHING TO DECLARE BUT LOVE"   No. 14

PAUL, ANGY *and* CHORUS

    ANGY *crosses with the* 1ST CUSTOMS OFFICER *to* R. *The* CHORUS *station themselves in three rows, the first in front of the downstage counter, the second on the downstage counter and the third on the second counter.* PAUL *watches* ANGY *whose back is resolutely turned to him.*

2ND CUSTOMS OFFICER [*over the music*] Anything to declare?
PAUL [*singing*]   I have nothing to declare,
                Nothing to declare but love.
                I have nothing to declare,
    ANGY, *surprised, turns and looks at Paul.*
                Nothing to declare but love.
    The CHORUS *turn and face up stage.*
                Search my heart; in my heart
                [*He crosses to Angy*]
                All I have is hidden there.
                Nothing to declare but love,
                But love, my love.
                [*He crosses to the 2nd Customs Officer*]
                Nothing in my pockets,
                Up my sleeve or in my glove.
    The CHORUS *turn.*
CHORUS.   No cigars, motor-cars.
PAUL [*moving* C] Just one thing I have acquired
                That I've plenty of,
                I mean my brand-new love.
                I have nothing to declare,
CHORUS.   Nothing to declare,
PAUL.   But love.
                I have nothing to declare
    ANGY *runs to Paul and puts her hand to his lips. He pulls her hand away and pulls her to him as she tries to get away.*
CHORUS.   Nothing to declare,
PAUL.   But love.
                Search my heart;

CHORUS.	in my heart,
PAUL.	All I have is hidden there.
CHORUS.	Nothing to declare,
PAUL.	But love.
CHORUS.	But love, my love.

ANGY releases herself and crosses to R.

PAUL and CHORUS.	I have nothing to declare,
	Nothing to declare but love.
	I have nothing to declare,
	Nothing to declare but love.
	Search my heart; in my heart
	All I have is hidden there.
	Nothing to declare but love,
	But love, my love.
ANGY.	I have nothing to declare,
	Nothing to declare.
PAUL.	Yes, you have and well you know it.
ANGY.	I swear.
PAUL.	But you're so afraid to show it.
	Tell me why?
ANGY.	I have nothing to declare,
	Nothing to declare.
PAUL.	Please don't waste another moment,
ANGY.	No, sir!
PAUL.	Let us live this precious moment while we may.
	Search your heart. Must you try to hide?
CHORUS.	Why don't you search your heart?
ANGY.	In my heart.
CHORUS.	Look inside your heart.
PAUL.	If you look deep down inside it,
	What is there?
ANGY.	There is nothing you can share.
CHORUS.	No.
ANGY.	Nothing hidden there.
CHORUS.	No, no, no, no.
ANGY.	I swear!
CHORUS.	No, no, no, no, no, no, no.
PAUL.	Be fair!
CHORUS.	No, no, no, no, no, no.
ANGY.	I swear!
CHORUS.	No, no, no, no.
ALL.	Nothing to declare but love!

PAUL exits down L. MARCELLE moves down to L of Angy.

MARCELLE. Angy, why are you so pale? You are trembling. Did they make you pay duty?
ANGY. Where's Dix? He was there a little while ago.
MARCELLE. He's probably trying to get a permit.
ANGY. Permit for what?
MARCELLE. To come inside and kiss the bride.
ANGY. Do you have to have a permit for that?
MARCELLE. This is a democratic country. You need a permit for everything.
ANGY. If I don't find him, I'll die. [*She moves R and looks out front*]

JACQUES enters L.

JACQUES. Allow me to save your life. I had no difficulty in finding him.

SCENE 7   WEDDING IN PARIS

                            DIXWOOD AIKEN *enters* L. *He is a solid young giant, extremely*   MUSIC
                            self-confident, a go-getter. His voice is enormous. He crosses
                            with ponderous steps and meets ANGY C.

DIX.   Angy!

                            FINALE ACT I   No. 15
                                CHORUS

                            As the CHORUS *sing,* DIX *embraces Angy, lifting her high. There*
                            is something so absurd in his youthful pomposity that MARCELLE
                            laughs and tosses a spiteful glance at Jacques.

CHORUS.   Nothing to declare but love.

                                CURTAIN

                            INTERMISSION MUSIC   No. 16

ACT II

SCENE 1

Marcelle's Garden. Morning

It is a garden with formal arrangements, clipped trees, and sculptured hedges behind a sedate Paris house, the entrance to which is R. *There is a long garden seat* RC *and a garden table and two chairs* LC.

PARIS BALLET   No. 17

DANCERS

When the CURTAIN *rises the* DANCERS *perform a ballet representing the Spirit of France.* MRS PILCHARD *is fussing around, supervising. The ballet ends with a picture.*

MRS PILCHARD. All right, girls. Hurry up and change.

The DANCERS *and* MRS PILCHARD *exit to the house* R.

A GUIDE *and the* TOURISTS *enter up* R. *The* GUIDE *is eager, impatient and business-like. He wears a cap marked in gilt letters* " HOOK'S TOURS ". *Some* TOURISTS *wear sun glasses, have cameras slung over their shoulders and read guide books. A few French Provincials, a couple of Germans, the majority of Americans with two G.I.'s. They group* C *around the Guide.*

GUIDE. Now, ladies and gentlemen—we are privileged and indebted to the present owner—Madame Thibault—to see here the loveliest private grounds in all Paris. You are standing on very historic soil. On the site of this magnificent edifice stood the Château de Foncelle. Towards the end of the eighteenth century the Marquis de Beaunais murdered his wife and seven children and burnt down the château to cover his crime. It was in these very grounds that Napoleon the First wandered and worked out his plan for the seige of Toulon. Now before I show you some of the relics associated with the Emperor of France, please come over here—[*he crosses down* L *and points out front*] and see from this vantage point the wonderful view of Paris second only to that from the Eiffel Tower. There you see the streets of Gay Paree.

" THE STREETS OF GAY PAREE "   No. 18

CHORUS

The TOURISTS *re-group and sing.*

CHORUS.   The streets of gay Paree,
             Nowhere else in all the world
             Could there be sights like these to see.
             From the Bois to Madeleine,
             And then at nights
             The lights
             Reflected in the Seine.
             Down at every street café
             Where youth and old roué
             Are flirting gaily
             Ev'ry night and ev'ry day.

             They vie and try to catch the eye
             Of all the ladies passing by
             Upon the streets of gay Paree.
             Where upon the Champs-Élysées

SCENE 1   WEDDING IN PARIS   33

> Lovers kiss beneath a tree,
> Let us meet where life is sweet
> And there is fun upon
> The streets of gay Paree.

MUSIC

GUIDE. Now come this way. Follow me and please keep to the paved paths and don't wander on the flower beds. I will first show you the stone bench on which Napoleon and Josephine spent many happy hours.

The GUIDE *and* TOURISTS, *chatting as they go, exit down* L.

JACQUES *and* DIX *enter from the house* R. JACQUES *has his arm around Dix's shoulders. They cross to the chairs* LC.

JACQUES. Well, how do you regard the proposition?
DIX. It's very gratifying to know that an executive of your calibre realizes that young blood makes an organization tick. [*He sits* R *of the table*]
JACQUES [*feeling for his cigarette case*] Please—sit down. [*He turns, sees Dix already seated and offers him the case*] Cigarette?

DIX *takes a cigarette.*

[*He lights Dix's cigarette*] Yes, we seem to be ticking regularly since the transfusion. [*He sits* L *of the table*] About sixteen months ago, wasn't it?
DIX [*rising*] Almost seventeen. Yes, sir, seventeen red-letter months in which I have had no thought save the Company's interest. Still, I had no idea that the executive office regarded me as such a valued employee.
JACQUES. You're too modest.
DIX [*crossing to* C] Youth is inclined to underestimate its worth. Take me, for instance. You think I knew that the great Monsieur Devallée was aware of my achievements? Or even my name?
JACQUES. You'd be surprised how much I know about you.
DIX. Of course, you were bound to hear about me sooner or later. When a young man has personality coupled with business acumen—[*he flicks his ash from his cigarette*] it's very difficult for him to remain a mere stooge in an overseas office.
JACQUES. Er—have you come to a decision?
DIX [*moving above the table*] Unequivocably affirmative. [*He flicks his ash which falls on Jacques*]
JACQUES. I am pleased. [*He picks up the ashtray and holds it out*]

DIX *drops his cigarette into the ashtray.*

Decision is the first step towards success. The second is action. You will be at the airport ready to take the plane for Canada at midnight.
DIX. Tonight?
JACQUES. Tonight.
DIX [*sitting* R *of the table*] Would a few days make such a difference, sir?
JACQUES. Is there any *personal* obstacle?
DIX. Well, sir . . .
JACQUES [*with studied indifference*] Yes?
DIX. Nothing very important.
JACQUES. No?
DIX. Just a fiancée. [*He crosses his legs*]
JACQUES. Oh! Congratulations. [*Innocently*] A Parisienne?
DIX. No, sir. She's a Canadian from my home town.
JACQUES. Then this will be a happy surprise for her.
DIX [*leaning forward*] But she's not in Canada, sir, she's here.
JACQUES [*with diabolic innocence*] In Paris?
DIX. She just arrived last night—on your ship. The *Queen Anne*.
JACQUES. Really? Who is she? Perhaps I know her.
DIX. Yes, sir, you do. You got me a pass to meet her. In fact she's staying in this house at the invitation of Madame Thibault.
JACQUES. Of course. But I thought she was your sister.

DIX. No, sir, my fiancée. I don't know how she'll like going right back to Saskatchewan tonight. MUSIC
JACQUES [*stricken*] You mean you'd take her back, too?
DIX. What else can I do with her?
JACQUES. I don't like to interfere in the personal lives of our future executives. Perhaps I ought to find some other young man for the job. [*He rises*]
DIX [*rising*] Oh, no, sir. I wouldn't let that stand in the way of my career. We both fly tonight.
JACQUES. Oh, that's dangerous.
DIX. In what way?
JACQUES. My dear boy, I know women. If you carry her off tonight you'll never hear the end of it. All your life she'll remind you that you robbed her of the chance to see Paris.
DIX. I'll show her Toronto.
JACQUES. I shouldn't if I were you. Wait, I have the solution. The company will be delighted to invite your fiancée for a fortnight's holiday in Paris.
DIX. No, sir, we can't allow that.
JACQUES. A wedding gift to a valued employee.
DIX. Well, that's another matter, sir.
JACQUES. The company insists. And I'll make it my personal business to see that she is not lonely. Good-bye. [*He shakes hands with Dix*]
DIX. I hate to bother you with petty details, sir.
JACQUES. But you don't know the French. We like nothing better than petty details.
DIX. Good-bye, sir, and thanks for *everything*.
JACQUES. Good luck to you, my boy.
DIX. And good luck to you, sir.

> JACQUES *and* DIX, *talking together, exit up* R.
> MARCELLE *enters up* L *and crosses to* C. *She is dressed in an elegant day dress and carries a basket of red roses.*
> A MAID *enters from the house.*

MAID. Madame. There is a gentleman from the Dominions Press Limited to see you. I told him to wait as you had arranged a special Press interview at twelve o'clock, but he insisted that as he was Dominions Press you would be pleased to give him an " exclusive " interview on your experiences in Canada.
MARCELLE. All right, Marie—I'll see him. [*She hands the basket to the Maid*] Take these in with you.
MAID. Yes, madame.

> *The* MAID *exits to the house* R.

GUIDE [*off up* L] Now keep close together, please, and keep to the stone paths.

> MARCELLE *moves quickly down* L *out of the sight of the* TOURISTS *who enter with the* GUIDE *up* L, *troop across the back and exit up* R.
> PAUL *enters from the house and crosses to* C.

PAUL. Marcelle.
MARCELLE [*crossing to* L *of Paul*] Paul.
PAUL. You can't escape the Press.
MARCELLE. It isn't for professional reasons that you're hounding me.
PAUL. We made a deal. Remember?
MARCELLE. I remember, but I'm not sure I can trust your intelligence.
PAUL. Would your intelligence allow you to tell me what Angy's doing?
MARCELLE. Crying.
PAUL. Why?
MARCELLE. How do I know? When the fiancé returned from his office he looked very grim in the face and said he must talk to Miss Dobson privately.
PAUL [*belligerently*] If that baboon doesn't treat her right . . .
MARCELLE. To treat her right he must marry her at once. Is that what you want?
PAUL [*crossing below Marcelle to* L] The poor kid doesn't know her own mind. She's been living in a dream.
MARCELLE. And has awakened in the arms of another man.
PAUL. Devallée? Has he been around yet?

SCENE 1   WEDDING IN PARIS

MARCELLE. Each time I hear the doorbell I make up my lips again. When the telephone rings I answer with my prettiest voice. And who is it?   MUSIC
PAUL. Who?
MARCELLE. You.
PAUL. I keep trying.
MARCELLE. It's no use. She will never talk to you again as long as she lives. And . . .
PAUL. And this time she means it.

The MAID *enters from the house.*

MAID. Excuse me, madame. The reporters have arrived.
MARCELLE. All right—I'll see them now.

The MAID *exits to the house.*

[*To Paul*] Although I have really nothing to declare.
PAUL. Not even love?
MARCELLE. At my age I am more interested in other people's love affairs.

ARCHER, BERMAN, COBB, DUVAL, EROTI *and* FRISCH, *newspaper reporters, enter from the house and surround Marcelle. They all have notebooks and pencils.*

ARCHER. Good afternoon, Madame Thibault—*London Sunday Journal.*
BERMAN. *New York Banner.*
COBB. *World Press Association.*
DUVAL. *Paris Midi.*
MARCELLE. Please. I have nothing to tell you.
DUVAL [*indicating Paul*] What have you revealed to *this* spy?
PAUL. She's not talking.
MARCELLE. For once we were not discussing my love life.
BERMAN. Oh, yeah!
COBB. Whose love life were you discussing?
MARCELLE [*pointing to Paul*] His.
REPORTERS [*laughing incredulously; ad lib.*] Paul? Has he any? Who's the dame? Give us a break, Paul. What's the story?
PAUL. I'd like to tell you, fellows, but it's not fit to print.

PAUL *crosses and exits up* R. *The* REPORTERS *crowd around Marcelle.*

DUVAL. Tell us, Madame Thibault, will you marry again this season?
FRISCH. Are Americans good lovers?
COBB. Is divorce on the upgrade or downswing?
BERMAN. Do you sleep in a nightgown or pyjamas?
MARCELLE. Boys, please—let me breathe.
REPORTERS [*together*] Talk.
MARCELLE. Very well, if you insist. I will give you my opinion on an important world topic—*Man.*

"A MAN IS A MAN IS A MAN"   No. 19

MARCELLE *and* REPORTERS

MARCELLE *sits* R *of the table* LC. *The* REPORTERS *group around he* .

MARCELLE. All around the world I've travelled,
Got my complexes unravelled,
Met a lot of men and married now and then.
REPORTERS. Lucky men!
MARCELLE. But in spite of where I've wandered
And of all the love I've squandered
I don't rue it,
I'd go through it all again.

REPORTERS. Not again?

MARCELLE. A man is a man is a man
And a woman takes a gamble in futurities,
Marrying security's
Part of every woman's plan
So marry the right kind of man.
Some men have sex, some may be wrecks,
But while they've got the strength to sign their cheques
Just get all you can, while you can,
And remember, men have chosen more seductive girls
Rather than productive girls.
Ever since the world began
A man is a man is a man.
[*She rises and crosses to* R]

The REPORTERS *follow to* L *of Marcelle.*

A man is a man is a man.
What d'you think he buys a mink to dress his honey for?
Keeps her flush with money for?
That's his egotistic plan
To keep her from some other man.
[*She advances on the Reporters*]

The REPORTERS *back to* LC.

Don't take abuse, don't be a goose,
There's always Reno where they turn you loose,
You must get the best from a man,
Though you have to snatch one
From the howling pack again.
When you hurl him back again
Then is when you start to plan
To find you a wealthier man.
[*She crosses below the Reporters to* L]

A man is a man is a man
And a woman has to bow to the inferior,
Make him feel superior,
If she wants to catch her man.
So flatter a man all you can.
First, they will stall, but when they fall,

The REPORTERS *take three steps towards Marcelle.*

They never know the woman's planned it all.
[*She advances on the Reporters*]

The REPORTERS *retire to* LC.

A man is a man is a man.
[*She crosses to* C]
In discussions of a honeymoon
You're soon immersed,
But they want rehearsals first.
Try to dodge it if you can,
Just don't let a man be a man,
A man is a man is a man.
When you meet and he's intrigued he wants to play with you,
But when he's been gay with you,

SCENE 1 WEDDING IN PARIS

		MUSIC

                  Suddenly he no can do,
                  And that's when the romance is through.
                  But when you're through, I'm telling you,
                  Don't lose the old until you find the new.
                  A man is a man is a man
                  And no matter what I have to say
                  About a man
                  I can't do without a man
                  Show me any girl who can,
                  A man is a man and I don't give a damn
REPORTERS.   'Cos a man is a man is a man
                  Is a man
ALL.   Is a man, is a man, is a man.

                            The REPORTERS *and* MARCELLE *exit to the house* R.
                            ANGY *and* DIX, *in earnest conversation, enter up* R.

ANGY [*moving up* L] . . . and no true woman would stand in the way of a man's career.
                            DIX *moves down* R.
But I wish you'd try to see my side of it. [*She moves* C]
  DIX [*moving to* R *of Angy*] I consider that downright selfish.
  ANGY. Did you hear what I said? That I'd die before I'd interfere with your career.
  DIX. I also heard you say you'd die if you had to leave Paris tonight.
  ANGY [*after a moment*] There's no other way, I guess. Whither thou goest . . . [*She crosses and sits* R *of the table* LC]
  DIX. I'm delighted with you. [*He crosses above the table* LC *to* L *of it*] Decision's the first step towards success.
  ANGY. But at least I'd like to see a few famous sights.
  DIX. You've got the rest of the day. [*He crosses below the table to* RC] While I'm packing and clearing up at the office.
  ANGY. Paris in half a day? After I've dreamed about it all my life?
  DIX. Wake up. Paris is just a city.
  ANGY [*rising and running to him*] Let's get going. We've still got twelve hours.
  DIX. But I've got to rest if we're going to fly all night.
  ANGY [*turning away and moving* C] Okay, I guess I'll have to see Paris by myself.

                      MARCELLE *enters from the house and crosses to Angy. She carries a spray of orchids.*

  MARCELLE. Excuse me interrupting you, darlings, but this has come for Angy.
  ANGY [*taking the orchids*] Oh, thank you, Dix.
  DIX. Huh?
  MARCELLE. Aren't you going to look at the card?
  ANGY [*reading*] "To the Paris bride, best wishes from International Grain and Cereal." Imagine them sending me orchids!
  MARCELLE. Imagine!
  DIX. International Grain and Cereal . . . ?
  MARCELLE [*crossing below Dix to* R *of him*] Generous of them, wasn't it?
  ANGY. Your friends in the office must think an awful lot of you.
  DIX. I don't get it. None of my friends knew.
  MARCELLE. Why? Were you keeping it a secret?
  DIX [*turning to Marcelle*] They'd have expected invitations to the wedding.
  MARCELLE. Naturally.
  DIX. It'd have cost a fortune.
  MARCELLE. Wouldn't it have been worth it?
  DIX. But it's the bride's folks who ought to pay for the wedding.
  MARCELLE. It's getting very close. I think there's a storm blowing up. [*She moves up* RC]
  ANGY. Dix, can't we be married informally this afternoon?

Dix. Not here.
Angy. Can't we?
Dix. It's not possible.
Angy. Dix, please. I'm willing to leave without seeing Napoleon's tomb, but I did want to be married in Paris.
Marcelle [*moving to* L *of the table* LC] It takes ten days here.
Dix [*crossing to* R *of the table* LC] You see, it's impossible.
Angy. All right. [*She fondles her orchids*] Anyway, I've had orchids. [*She sits on the seat* RC]

The Maid *enters from the house.*

Maid. Excuse me, madame—that exclusive gentleman from the Press wishes to see Mademoiselle Dobson.
Angy [*rising*] Not Dominions Press?
Marcelle. Isn't that the service that sends news to the Canadian papers?
Angy. How did they know I was here?
Marcelle. Newspaper men are clever. [*To the Maid*] Ask him to come through. [*She moves up* C]

The Maid *exits to the house.*

Dix. Well, I never thought they'd bother to interview you.
Marcelle. Maybe they heard that you were here.
Dix. Yeah!

Paul *enters from the house. He carries Marcelle's red roses.*

Paul [*crossing to* R *of Marcelle*] How do you do?
Marcelle. How do you do? [*She shakes hands with Paul*] How nice to see you.
Paul [*moving to* L *of Angy*] Felicitations to the happy bride. [*He gives Angy the bouquet*]
Angy. Thank you.
Dix [*moving* C] I suppose you have come to interview me about the wedding?

Angy *puts her flowers on the seat* RC.

Marcelle [*crossing below Dix to the table* LC] Excuse me! [*She busies herself setting the chairs* LC *into the table*]
Paul. I'd like a few words——
Dix. Well, now . . .
Paul. —from Miss Dobson.
Angy. I have nothing to say.
Paul. Nothing at all? No first impressions?
Angy. I've only been here since last night and I haven't left this house.
Dix. I've got a piece of news for your papers. Miss Dobson and I aren't getting married in Paris.
Marcelle [*sitting* R *of the table* LC] What?
Paul. You're not?
Dix. Business makes it imperative that I leave at once—I'm with International Grain.
Marcelle. Have you been promoted?
Dix [*crossing above the seat* RC *to* R *of Angy*] You bet.

Marcelle *laughs.*

Paul [*to Angy*] When are you leaving?
Angy. Tonight.
Paul. That must be a great disappointment.
Dix [*putting his arm around Angy*] We're the happiest couple in the world.
Marcelle. Where've I heard that before?
Paul. How do you feel about it—Miss Dobson?
Angy. It's a great opportunity for Dixwood.
Dix [*crossing to* L *of Paul*] We'll be married in Hitchemup, Saskatchewan, in my parents' backyard.
Angy. In your backyard?
Dix. Yours is too small.

MARCELLE. Oh, what a pity!
DIX [*to Marcelle*] I'd like you to see our home. [*He indicates with a wide sweeping gesture*] Dad's got some of the finest acreage in Saskatchewan.
MARCELLE [*very solemnly*] I'm so glad.

PAUL *crosses above Dix and Marcelle to* L *of the table* LC.

DIX. He'll string up Japanese lanterns and my Mom'll bake the wedding cake.
ANGY [*moving to* R *of Dix*] I think my mother'd want to do that.
MARCELLE [*rising, crossing and standing below the garden seat* RC] But naturally.
DIX [*crossing to* L *of Marcelle*] Whose mother won baking prizes at the County Fair?
MARCELLE. I haven't the slightest idea.
DIX [*turning to Angy*] You remember Mom's Mock Angel Cake, Angy, and her banana pie?
MARCELLE [*with a hand to her stomach*] Not banana pie!

PAUL *sits* L *of the table* LC.

DIX [*moving up* C] Many a night I've dreamed of Mom's banana pie.
ANGY. And I've dreamed of Paris. [*She crosses to* L *of Marcelle and kneels on the seat* RC] But it's not just the wedding, is it? It's the one you marry. He's for life.
DIX. You said it.
PAUL. So choose the right one. Or you're stuck.
MARCELLE. If you're marrying for love, Angy, make sure it's the real thing. There's no worse agony than the first divorce.

MARCELLE *exits to the house.*

DIX [*moving down* C] There'll never be a divorce in our family.
PAUL. Let that be a warning.
ANGY [*sitting on the seat* RC] But how can you be wrong about someone you've known all your life —since you were in school?
DIX. You can't.
PAUL. We leave school when we grow up. And sometimes the childhood dreams turn out to be banana pie.
ANGY. I wish you'd leave now.
DIX. Angela! Please! [*To Paul*] If you want my impressions of Paris after——
PAUL }
DIX   } [*together*] —sixteen months, three weeks and eleven days . . .
DIX. Huh?
ANGY. Please go.
DIX. How can you be so rude? This chap's come here to do his job . . .
ANGY [*to Paul*] Please.
PAUL [*rising and crossing to Angy*] Can I come back?
ANGY. I won't be here. Good-bye.

PAUL *moves to the house door* R *and turns.*

PAUL [*to Dix*] Bye-bye, banana pie.

PAUL *exits to the house.*

DIX. The smart type! But you shouldn't have lost your temper. I could have given him a great story.
ANGY [*rising and crossing to Dix; with sudden fury*] Don't be so smug.
DIX. You've certainly changed, Angela Emily Dobson.
ANGY. So have you.
DIX. I never change.
ANGY. Perhaps you don't. [*She moves to* L *of the seat* RC] Perhaps you're the same boy we used to cheer at football games, still waiting for cheers.
DIX. Women are always nervous when they have to change their plans. I advise a good rest before we get on that plane tonight.

JACQUES *enters from the house and crosses to* C.

JACQUES. Good morning.
DIX [*moving to* L *of Jacques*] Why, Monsieur Devallée! What an honour.
JACQUES. I called to see how your fiancée was getting on.
DIX. How very kind, Monsieur Devallée. This is Angy . . .
JACQUES. Yes, I know. We have met.
ANGY. Thank you very much for the orchids, *Jacques*. And for giving Dix that new job.
JACQUES. I hoped you'd be pleased.
ANGY. He's terribly happy about going back to Saskatchewan.
DIX. So is Angy. Much more thrilled than she'll let on.
JACQUES. Not half so thrilled as she will be when I have shown her Paris.
ANGY. Oh, will you? We've got just twelve hours and Dix wants to sleep.
JACQUES. I beg your pardon! We have two weeks.
ANGY. But how, if I leave at midnight?
JACQUES [*to Dix*] Haven't you told her?
ANGY. What?
DIX. It was just an idea.
ANGY. What kind of idea?
DIX. It doesn't matter now that you've decided to leave with me tonight. [*He circles the chairs and table* LC]
ANGY. What idea?
JACQUES. I suggested to your fiancé that you might enjoy a two weeks' holiday in Paris as a guest of the company.
ANGY. You did!
DIX. I knew you wouldn't accept.
ANGY. *How* did you know?
JACQUES. Yes, how did you know?
DIX. What would people say?
JACQUES. What people?
DIX. Hitchemup.
ANGY. They'd say I was having a wonderful time in Paris.
DIX. Think of my mother. What'd she say?
ANGY. Tell her to bake a banana pie. [*She turns her back to Dix and stands below the seat* RC]
DIX. Well, if that's the way you feel, I'm going. [*He starts to cross above Jacques to the house door* R]
JACQUES [*catching his arm*] Just a minute.

DIX *stops* R *of Jacques.*

I think we ought to clarify the situation. [*He moves down* LC] Does this mean the engagement is broken?

ANGY *is silent*

DIX. I'm not in a position to answer that question. It's the lady's privilege. [*He moves to* L *of Angy*] I must say I'm deeply hurt by the heartless frivolity of a woman I thought was as true as the stars above.
ANGY [*turning*] All I said was that I didn't want to get married in your backyard. [*She crosses to Jacques*] Do you think I'm frivolous?
DIX [*following to* R *of Angy*] Of course he does. You realize your disloyalty to me will be front-page news back home?
ANGY. I'm not disloyal, but there are other people to think of.
DIX. Who?
ANGY. Hitchemup! Why else did they buy me that first-class ticket on the *Queen Anne*? If I'm not going to be married here, at least I owe it to them to see Paris. [*To Jacques*] If you still want to show me.
DIX. No, I won't allow it. We can't take advantage of Monsieur Devallée's generosity.
JACQUES. Oh, yes, you can. Miss Dobson, it will give me great pleasure . . .
DIX. Well—you're the boss, sir.
JACQUES [*crossing to* L *of Dix*] But it's young blood like yours that makes an organization tick.
DIX. Thank you, sir. I'm more than gratified. But I'm afraid you'll find Angy too much trouble.
JACQUES. Trouble is a gentleman's privilege.
DIX [*slapping Jacques heartily on the back*] Then I accede to your gentlemanly suggestion.

SCENE 2   WEDDING IN PARIS

JACQUES. Hadn't you better start packing?   MUSIC
DIX. At once, sir. [*He moves above the seat* RC] My fiancée and I would like to express our gratitude to International Grain and Cereal. [*He moves to the house door* R *and turns*] We'll say good-bye later, Angy.

DIX exits quickly to the house.

JACQUES [*turning to Angy*] Well?
ANGY [*running to him*] You're really going to show me Paris?
JACQUES. Of course.
ANGY. I can't wait. There's a sightseeing bus at one-thirty.
JACQUES. A *bus*!
ANGY. You see more that way quicker.
JACQUES. But I have my car.
ANGY [*doubtfully*] Would you know where to go?
JACQUES. I was born here.
ANGY. Have you ever been up the Eiffel Tower?
JACQUES. No.
ANGY. Or to the Flea Market?
JACQUES. Yes.
ANGY. Or the Sewers of Paris?
JACQUES. Heaven forbid!
ANGY. Then I'm going to take you on some *proper* tours with a guide and everything. Let's get going.
JACQUES. But it's lunch-time. Let's eat first.
ANGY. We'll buy sandwiches and eat them on the bus.
JACQUES. Sandwiches on the bus!
ANGY. Okay?
JACQUES. Okay!

JACQUES *takes* ANGY'S *hand and they exit to the house as the lights*
BLACK-OUT *and*

LIGHTING CUE 16

the RUNNING TABS *close*

SCENE 2

A Paris Street

The setting is a front-cloth depicting a typical Paris street, the kiosk with advertisements, the café awning, the chestnut trees and all such cosy and distinctive bits.

"TOURIST SONG"   No. 20

LA TOULOUSE, MRS PILCHARD *and* CHORUS

When the RUNNING TABS *open, the* TOURISTS, *led by the* GUIDE, *enter* L *and sing.* MRS PILCHARD *is with them.*

CHORUS.   Go to Paris, you must see Paris,
               You have not lived till you've seen Paree,
               Said the boasters and tourist posters,
               And so we came to see.
               Prudes and purists become gay tourists
               When they arrive on a tourist plane.
               Once alighted, they get excited,
               At the first sight of the Seine.

               C'est Paree, c'est Paree, c'est Paree,
               We're the tourists you see marching round and round.

	C'est la vie, c'est la vie de Paree.
	Then at night we all go out and paint the town.
	We can spend a moonlit hour
	Climbing up the Eiffel Tower,
	Then we'll see gay Paree from above.
	When we've seen the Exhibitions,
	And we've lost our inhibitions,
	Only Paris is the place to fall in love.

LA TOULOUSE enters.

LA TOULOUSE. Land for lovers, city of laughter,
Made for pleasure, take all it can give.
Once you've seen it, then ever after
You will love Paris, see Paris and live.

LA TOULOUSE exits.

CHORUS. Land for lovers, city of laughter,
Made for pleasure, take all it can give.
Once you've seen it, then ever after
You will love Paris, see Paris and live.

MRS PILCHARD. Up and down the Rivoli, and all around the Tuileries,
Place Vendôme, and Notre-Dame, and in and out the galleries,
Morning, noon and night we march in motion that's perpetual,
On the move and in the Louvre, getting intellectual.
Cabarets in many ways appealing to the sensual,
Going to the Follies, where the girls are three dimensional,
From the Concorde to the Étoile, Invalides and Madeleine,
Tourists go insane beside the Seine.

ALL. C'est Paree, c'est Paree, c'est Paree,
We're the tourists you see marching round and round.
C'est la vie, c'est la vie de Paree.
Then at night we all go out and paint the town.
We can spend a moonlit hour
Climbing up the Eiffel Tower,
Then we'll see gay Paree from above.
When we've seen the Exhibitions,
And we've lost our inhibitions,
Only Paris is the place to fall in love.
C'est Paree, c'est Paree, ça c'est Paree.

The FRONT CLOTH rises

SCENE 3

A Paris Boulevard

Across the back are two outdoor cafés on either side of the double doors of an office building with plaques that show the names of the businesses inside. Most conspicuous of these is a plaque that reads, " DOMINIONS PRESS LTD *". The cafés* R *and* L *are furnished with the usual outdoor tables and chairs.*

When the FRONT-CLOTH *rises, the* TOURISTS *merge into the scene. The* GUIDE *counts the Tourists.*

GUIDE. One couple is missing.

ANGY enters R.

ANGY [*apologetically*] We just stopped to look at a place where some of Monsieur Devallée's ancestors were beheaded.
GUIDE. Don't let it happen again.

SCENE 3 WEDDING IN PARIS

ANGY. Okay!
GUIDE [*to the Tourists*] And now we complete today's tour with a visit to the monument of Madame Pompadour's brother. [*He crosses to* L]
ANGY [*calling off* R] Jacques! The tomb of Madame Pompadour's brother.

> JACQUES *enters* R, *limping and looking really worn out. The* GUIDE *exits* L. *The* TOURISTS *follow him off.* ANGY *starts to follow, but* JACQUES *detains her.*

JACQUES. I've walked round Paris eight hours a day for two weeks. I want to sit down and have an aperitif. [*He calls*] Garçon. Garçon.
ANGY [*moving* C] Oh, well. [*She looks around*] Just pure glamour. Millions of people dream all their lives and never see it and here I am with Paris at my feet.
JACQUES [*sitting* L *of the table* RC] My feet hurt. [*He puts his hat on the table*]
ANGY. But think of all the art and beauty we've covered in two weeks. [*She crosses and sits above the table* RC]
JACQUES. If we'd covered it in my car we'd have had time for civilized meals as well.
ANGY. What can you see from a Rolls Royce?

> *The* WAITER *enters up* R *and comes to* L *of Jacques.*

WAITER. Monsieur—dame?
JACQUES. Bon jour. Apportez moi deux bout . . .

> ANGY *looks at Jacques.*

Two Coca-Cola.
WAITER. Oui, Monsieur.

> *The* WAITER *exits up* R.

ANGY. After I'm gone I bet you'll never look at another historic monument.
JACQUES. Every monument in Paris will be a shrine to the memory of your visit.
ANGY. I love it when you tease me. [*She stretches her hand out over the table*]

> JACQUES *holds Angy's hand and kisses it.*

But how will you really feel when I'm gone?
JACQUES. I'll look back on your visit as one of the most amazing experiences of my life.
ANGY. I can't bear it to end. Oh, Jacques! [*She puts her arm around his shoulders*]

> *The* WAITER *enters up* R *with two opened bottles of Coca-Cola and two straws. He puts them on the table* RC, *then exits up* R.

JACQUES. When you look back on it, Angy, how will you think of the middle-aged man who showed you Paris?
ANGY. Don't always talk like that. You're younger than a lot of people. Dix, for instance. He acts like your grandfather.
JACQUES. Sssh! Don't shout, it makes me nervous.
ANGY. Do you know he hasn't bothered to send me one postcard in two weeks.
JACQUES. Shall I phone Marcelle and ask if a letter has come?
ANGY. If I never hear from him again, it'll be too soon.
JACQUES. You amaze me, Angy. I always thought you were very faithful.
ANGY. Do *you* want me to be?
JACQUES. Angy, I don't want to hurt you, but . . .
ANGY. How could you? You've been better to me than anyone in my whole life. [*She clasps him around the neck, picks up a bottle, takes a drink, then offers it to Jacques*]

> JACQUES *shudders and waves the bottle aside.*

JACQUES. Aren't you hungry? Where would you like to eat?
ANGY. Please, do I have to eat one of those big fancy meals? I'd like just a sandwich. Right here if you don't mind.
JACQUES. As you wish. But first I'll telephone Marcelle and ask if any letters have come for you. [*He rises*] Can you order the sandwiches? Another sandwich! I'm beginning to look like a sandwich.
D

WEDDING IN PARIS

"HOW DO I KNOW IT'S LOVE?"
ANGY, GIRLS and DANCERS

Music No. 21

JACQUES exits by the double doors up C. *ANGY falls into a reverie for a few moments, then sings.*

ANGY. How do I know it's love?
I must be sure it's love.
Will someone come to guide me,
My dream appear beside me?
Maybe I'll see a sign,
Shine like a star above,
Although I know my heart says it's so,
How do I know it's love?
[*She rises and moves down* R]

The GIRLS, *in couples, drift slowly on* R *and* L, *group and listen to Angy.*

Love's a state of mind,
And all who love are blind,
I know too well.
[*She crosses to* C]
But as far as my heart is concerned,
There's so much, and so little, I've learned.
So two people meet
And hearts forget to beat,
But who can tell
If it's true,
How I wish that I knew.

The GIRLS *vocalize.*

How do I know it's love?
I must be sure it's love.
Will someone come to guide me,
My dream appear beside me?
Maybe I'll see a sign,
Shine like a star above,
Although I know my heart says it's so,
How do I know it's love?

The DANCERS *enter from the café up* L *and dance with* ANGY *to a repeat of the number. The* GIRLS *sing the final refrain.*

GIRLS. How do I know it's love?
I must be sure it's love.
Will someone come to guide me,
My dream appear beside me?
Maybe I'll see a sign,
Shine like a star above.
Ah!

During the last two lines, the DANCERS *and* GIRLS *exit.*

ANGY. Although I know my heart says it's so,
How do I know it's love?

ANGY sits L *of the table* RC.

PAUL enters by the double doors up C. *He does not notice Angy and sits* R *of the table* LC.

The WAITER *enters up* R *and crosses to* R *of Paul.*

SCENE 3] WEDDING IN PARIS

PAUL. Bon jour, Louis. Donnez moi . . .   MUSIC
WAITER. Hamburger et café.
PAUL. Oui, merci.
                                    The WAITER *crosses to the table* RC.
WAITER. Madame désire encore quelque chose ?
                                    PAUL *looks up and sees Angy.*
ANGY. Yes. Oui. [*She struggles with the language*] Deux sandwiches, s'il vous plait. Jambon et . . .
PAUL. Jambon et fromage.
ANGY. Oui, jambon et . . . [*She breaks off, looks around, sees Paul and rises. To the waiter*] No, no. J'ai changé mon tête. [*She moves down* R]
                                    The WAITER *exits up* R.
PAUL [*rising*] Why don't you sit down and wait for your sandwiches ? You can change your head quietly. I thought you'd gone back to Canada.
ANGY. I stayed to see Paris.
PAUL [*crossing to her*] Why didn't you give me a ring ? You knew where to find me.
                                    ANGY *is silent.*
Why not ?
ANGY. I haven't had the time.
PAUL. What's kept you so busy ?
ANGY. The Bastille, Sacré Cœur, the Café de Paris, Maxim's—the bridges of the Seine, the Hôtel de Ville, *Folies Bergère* and Père Lachaise Cemetery.
PAUL. What's left for me to show you ?
ANGY. We still have Malmaison, Fontainebleau and the night tour of the Louvre with floodlighting.
PAUL. If that's what you want, you've got an escort.
ANGY. Thanks, but we've already booked our places.
PAUL. We ? So your fiancé stayed in Paris. [*He crosses to* C]
                                    ANGY *does not reply and half-turns her back to him.*
[*He turns*] Gave up the Canadian job ?
                                    ANGY *is still mute.*
Are you married yet ?
ANGY. No.
PAUL. When's the wedding ?
                                    ANGY *shrugs her shoulders.*
You haven't changed your mind, have you ?
                                    There is a long silence.
[*He crosses to her*] Still scared ?
ANGY [*turning on him*] What have I to be afraid of ?
PAUL. The truth—naked and unashamed.
ANGY. I don't know what you're talking about.
PAUL [*moving* C] Most of us would rather see ourselves as dressed-up dream people than look straight at our unflattering nakedness.
ANGY. Well, what's so wrong about me naked ?
PAUL. You want to be a martyr. You'd cut off your hand. You'd burn at the stake. You'd—you'd marry a man you've quit loving . . .
ANGY [*crossing to him*] What makes you think I have quit loving him ?
PAUL. You'd have left him the day you got here if you hadn't been afraid it was disloyal to love another man.
ANGY. That's the most conceited remark I have ever heard from the male sex.
PAUL [*crossing below her to* RC] You needn't think I'm being personal.

ANGY [*following him*] I wouldn't care if you were. If you want my opinion of you stark naked . . .   MUSIC
PAUL. What is your opinion ?
ANGY. You're more conceited than that Saskatchewan Romeo and I wouldn't marry you if you were the last man on earth.

The WAITER *enters up* R *with the coffee and hamburger, crosses and puts it on the table* LC.

PAUL. Did anyone ask you ?
ANGY [*turning her back on him*] Don't bother.
WAITER [*calling*] Monsieur, votre 'amburger, votre café.
PAUL. Oh, you eat 'em.

PAUL *crosses and exits down* L.

The WAITER *leaves the tray on the table* LC *and exits up* R. ANGY *looks after Paul for a few moments, then sits* L *of the table* RC.

JACQUES *enters by the double doors up* C. *He carries a slip of paper.*

JACQUES [*moving to* L *of Angy*] Angy, Angy. A cable from Dix.
ANGY. From Saskatchewan ? How'd you get it ?
JACQUES [*handing her the slip of paper*] Marcelle gave it to me on the phone. Can you read my writing ?
ANGY [*reading with difficulty*] " Cancel sailing—take . . . " What's the next word ?
JACQUES [*reading*] " Cancel sailing. Take first plane. Imperative you here by the fifteenth. Mother's anniversary. Wedding same date. Dix."
ANGY. He didn't even say " love ".
JACQUES [*moving to the doors up* C] I'll get you a reservation on the plane.
ANGY [*rising and crossing to* LC] Please, don't always try to make decisions for me. I know my own mind.
JACQUES [*moving down* C] But you will have to fly back.
ANGY. No.
JACQUES. To be there by the fifteenth . . .
ANGY [*turning to him*] I won't be there by the fifteenth, *nor* the sixteenth—*nor* the seventeenth. I am *not* going to be married on his mother's anniversary, and I am not going to be married in his old backyard. [*She pauses briefly*] I have given up my loyalty to Dixwood Aiken.
JACQUES. I admire your spirit, but please think again.
ANGY. I've got to send a cable to Dix. [*She starts to go*]
JACQUES [*detaining her*] No, you must never send a cable in such a hurry—you must think it over calmly.
ANGY. What's there to think about ? I've made a decision.
JACQUES. What—er—what are you going to do ? [*He crosses to the table* RC *and picks up a bottle of Coca-Cola in his right hand*]
ANGY. Marry you.

JACQUES *is dumbfounded. He stares at Angy, baffled.*

[*She crosses to the table* RC] Come along, dear. We must be going. Put on your hat, dear.

JACQUES *lifts the bottle to drink.*

[*She picks up Jacques' hat and puts it on his head*] Isn't it a wonderful feeling when everything's settled ?

ANGY *pulls* JACQUES *by the right arm, drawing the bottle away and leaving the straw in his mouth, and drags him off down* R.

The WAITER *enters up* R, *moves to the table* RC *and collects the second Coca-Cola bottle.*

PAUL *enters down* L.

PAUL. Garçon, what happened to the young lady ?
WAITER. The one you were shouting at, Monsieur ? She's just gone off with a gentleman. Shall I try and catch them ?
PAUL. Leave it.

"I MUST HAVE BEEN CRAZY"

PAUL

The WAITER *exits up* R. PAUL *sits* R *of the table* LC.

MUSIC
No. 22

PAUL. I must have been crazy,
To ever think that you could be in love with me.
I must have been crazy,
When I believed
What in my heart I know was never so.
Now go, go on and leave me,
Don't break the rule,
But make a fool of someone new.
Me, I must be crazy
Because I love you and you know I do.
[*He rises and moves down* C]

The RUNNING TABS *close behind Paul*

When we are young and so romantic,
It's easy to fall in love.
We fell in love, nor reasoned why,
Only to find our love a lie.
No tears to be shed,
Only this to be said.

I must have been crazy,
To ever think that you could be in love with me.
I must have been crazy,
When I believed
What in my heart I know was never so.
Now go, go on and leave me,
Don't break the rule,
But make a fool of someone new.
Me, I must be crazy
Because I love you and you know I do.

The lights BLACK-OUT.

LIGHTING CUE 17

SCENE 4

Jacques' Library

The scene is an inset with the door R. *There is a small console table* C *with armchairs* R *and* L *of it. When the* RUNNING TABS *open,* JACQUES *is curled miserably in the armchair* L. *The* BUTLER *enters.*

BUTLER. A lady to see you, Monsieur.

JACQUES, *frozen, does not respond.*

[*He gives a little cough. Louder*] Lady to see you, Monsieur.
JACQUES. Huh?
BUTLER. Shall I ask her to come in?
JACQUES. No, no, no, I'm not at home.

MARCELLE *enters.*

MARCELLE. Forgive me for bursting in on you. When I heard the good news I couldn't restrain myself.

The BUTLER *exits.*

JACQUES. What news?
MARCELLE. Angy's just told me. I simply had to come and congratulate you.
JACQUES. What's Angy told you?
MARCELLE. Darling, for an engaged man you don't sound very enthusiastic. [*She removes her stole, and finding nowhere to put it, throws it over Jacques*]
JACQUES. I've never been so happy in my life. [*He puts the stole over the arm of his chair*]
MARCELLE. I'm so glad. May I sit down?

JACQUES *acquiesces*.

[*She sits in the armchair* R] I could hardly believe it when I heard that you were thinking seriously of marriage.
JACQUES. Why not? Marriage is a serious affair.
MARCELLE. If it were only a serious affair, I'd give you my blessing. But for a man who has so carefully kept himself a bachelor to change his habits so abruptly . . .
JACQUES. Do you find anything wrong—perverse—abnormal—about a man changing his habits?
MARCELLE. Still, it's remarkable after all these years that you've decided to marry a girl of Angy's age.
JACQUES. Many mature men are attracted by an excess of youth.
MARCELLE. It'll be like teaching a young niece the alphabet. But of course, very stimulating.
JACQUES. I look forward to it with great emotion.
MARCELLE. She'll cling to you forever.
JACQUES. Will she?
MARCELLE. You'll never be out of her sight.
JACQUES. What a comfort you are.
MARCELLE [*rising and crossing to him*] And don't forget, dear, when you have your first little matrimonial problems come straight to me. My experience is always at your service.
JACQUES. I'm deeply grateful.
MARCELLE. May I have a little drinkie?
JACQUES. Yes.

MARCELLE *turns to the table and pours a glass of sherry for herself*.

MARCELLE. Now, firstly, I'll find someone to take this delightful apartment off your hands . . .
JACQUES. I don't intend to move out of it.

MARCELLE *drinks and puts the glass on the tray*.

MARCELLE. Don't be silly, darling. Angy'll want something quite different. More functional. Canadians are quite advanced—in some ways. And you'll need a room for her mother. Naturally she'll live with you—has she a maiden aunt? I believe they do, too. A couple of rooms will do for the children—to start with.

JACQUES *laughs almost hysterically*.

But, darling, surely you want a nice cosy family life. [*She turns to him and strokes his hair*]
JACQUES. I don't want anything of the kind. [*He starts to leap out of the chair*]
MARCELLE [*pressing him back into the chair*] Jacques dear, calm yourself, calm yourself. You're suffering the nerves of a young lover. You'll feel better when the engagement celebrations are over. [*She picks up her stole and throws it at him to put on for her*] I'm arranging a little party for you and Angy on Thursday night.
JACQUES [*rising*] I never go to parties. [*He puts Marcelle's stole around her shoulders*]
MARCELLE. You will now. At Angy's age one is taken to parties every night. Once you've introduced her to some of your friends, you'll be staying up until five—six o'clock every morning.
JACQUES. Please . . .
MARCELLE. Followed by a brisk canter in the Bois, before a hearty Canadian breakfast of sausages and treacle.
JACQUES. You must join us some morning.
MARCELLE. Alas, at our age it isn't wise to appear before luncheon. [*Her voice softens*] Then we'd drive along the Seine to Fontainebleau—a little rest before a cosy dinner—the ballet, perhaps—some quiet music of our own choosing—and so to bed.
JACQUES. You make it sound enchanting.

MARCELLE. It would have been. [*She moves to the door*] Au'voir.
  MARCELLE *exits*. JACQUES' *eyes are bright again, and his old gay spirit is back.*
JACQUES [*with a step towards the door*] **Marcelle** . . .
  But MARCELLE *has gone.*

" STRIKE ANOTHER MATCH "

No. 23

JACQUES

JACQUES. I have tried to use a modicum of philosophy,
With the ladies who've considered me quite a catch,
For I've always learned before you burn your fingers,
Strike another match.

When I had a funny feeling that I was weakening,
And I thought I might be softening in the thatch,
I recall I learned before you burn your fingers,
Strike another match.
[*He moves down* C]

  The RUNNING TABS *close behind Jacques.*

So many lovely girls I've met
Who've set my heart aglow,
But just the same a fellow has to know
When to say no.

I'll admit I've had a struggle to keep my sanity,
When they dimmed the light and quietly slid the latch,
But I've always learned before you burn your fingers,
Strike another match.

My married friends all tell me I should marry,
From bachelordom they've tried converting me,
But is it 'cause they want to see me happy,
Or the fact that misery loves company?

I've met a lot of ladies in my travels,
Redheads, brunettes and blondes and in between,
Yes, many a girl I've met who's young and forty,
And many an older girl of seventeen.
The young ones and others,
Egged on by fond mothers,
To tell us how much we must need 'em
When you've nothing to gain
But a ball and a chain,
And you've nothing to lose but your freedom.

I have tried to use a modicum of philosophy,
With the ladies who've considered me quite a catch,
For I've always learned before you burn your fingers,
Strike another match.

When I had a funny feeling that I was weakening,
And I thought I might be softening in the thatch,
I recall I learnt before you burn your fingers,
Strike another match.

The women are the hunters now,
And men their lawful prey,
But I'm the one that took the bait
And always got away.

I'll admit I've had a struggle to keep my sanity,
When they dimmed the light and quietly slid the latch,
But I've always learned before you burn your fingers,
[*He mimes striking a match on the sole of his shoe and blowing it out*]
Strike another match.

    The lights BLACK-OUT.

LIGHTING CUE 18

SCENE 5
Marcelle's Garden. Evening

An ornate tent has been erected L *and the garden is lit by Chinese lanterns.*

PINK BALLET   No. 24
DANCERS

When the RUNNING TABS *open, the* GUESTS *are assembled, watching the ballet. The* DANCERS *in bright shades of pink ; the girls in lighter shades ; the men in tails, with pink carnations in their buttonholes.*

At the end of the ballet, the DANCERS *exit up* L *and up* R.

"IN THE PINK"   No. 25
MARCELLE *and* CHORUS

  MARCELLE, *with a* GENTLEMAN *as escort, enters from the house and comes down* C. *The* CHORUS *dance.*

MARCELLE. Ev'ryone is dancing,
Love is in the air.
Nights of gladness are all too rare,
But tonight I'm happy.
Though the moments fly,
Let me tell you the reason why.

My heart's as light as air tonight,
There's music everywhere tonight,
I haven't got a care tonight,
For I am in the pink.

Perhaps because it's Spring again,
I want to have my fling again,
I want to dance and sing again,
For I am in the pink.

I know my eyes are glowing,
With joy I'm overflowing,
My heart is light, I'm fine tonight,
And ev'rything's divine tonight,
For all the world is mine tonight,
And I am in the pink.

  MARCELLE *dances with her* ESCORT.

SCENE 5 WEDDING IN PARIS

CHORUS.	My heart's as light as air tonight,	MUSIC
	There's music ev'rywhere tonight,	
	I haven't got a care tonight,	
MARCELLE.	For I am in the pink.	
GIRLS.	La, la, la, la, la, la, la, la.	
CHORUS.	Perhaps because it's Spring again,	
	I want to have my fling again,	
	I want to dance and sing again,	
MARCELLE and CHORUS.	For I am in the pink.	
MARCELLE.	I know my eyes are glowing,	
	With joy I'm overflowing,	
CHORUS.	My heart is light, I'm fine tonight,	
	And ev'rything's divine tonight,	
	For all the world is mine tonight,	
MARCELLE and CHORUS.	And I am in the pink.	

The GUESTS *disperse upstage in various groups and gradually exit during the ensuing dialogue. Marcelle's* ESCORT *stands by the garden seat* LC.

MRS PILCHARD *enters from the house and meets* MARCELLE RC. *They shake hands.*

MRS PILCHARD. Bon jour! Comment vous portez vous?
MARCELLE. I carry myself very well, thank you. How good of you to come.
MRS PILCHARD. I was mighty glad to be invited. Such a lovely place. [*She crosses below Marcelle to* C] So authentic.
MARCELLE [*moving down* R] Louis-Philippe.
MRS PILCHARD. Really? You must give me his address.
MARCELLE. I'm not quite certain where he is just now.
MRS PILCHARD. On the left bank. [*She moves* RC] All the bright boys are over there. Painters, musicians, bartenders—and all those students, dear. Ah! Paris! Home of love and lovers.
MARCELLE [*indicating her Escort* LC] You'll find Monsieur Leclerc a typical Parisian. [*To her Escort*] Henri, will you take Mrs Pilchard to the bar?
MRS PILCHARD. Dee-lighted. [*To Marcelle*] Thank you.

MRS PILCHARD *takes the arm of the handsome young man, rolls her eyes and exits with him* L. MARCELLE *turns towards the house door.*

JACQUES *enters up* R *and meets* MARCELLE RC.

JACQUES. I must congratulate you. Your party has great style. [*He takes Marcelle's hand and kisses it*]
MARCELLE [*walking round him to display her dress*] I hoped to impress you.
JACQUES. You have.
MARCELLE. With your dislike of parties I was afraid you wouldn't come.
JACQUES. I expect to have a wonderful time before the evening's over. But I'm afraid I must ask you to excuse me for a little while. [*He turns towards the house door*]
MARCELLE [*detaining him*] So soon? The party's only just begun.
JACQUES. I shan't be long. I've some business to attend to.
MARCELLE. At this late hour?
JACQUES. It's not exactly business. Just something I must fetch for Angy.
MARCELLE. Can't your chauffeur do it?
JACQUES. No, this is something I must take care of myself. It's to be a surprise.
MARCELLE. An engagement present?
JACQUES. Yes, you might call it that. [*He starts to back away*]

MARCELLE *holds and detains Jacques.*

E

                                    MELOS

MARCELLE [*over the music*] I also have a surprise for Angy.
JACQUES. How charming of you.
                        MARCELLE *and* JACQUES *dance.*
MARCELLE. I've grown fond of Angy. She's almost like a daughter to me.
JACQUES. You'll make an enchanting mother-in-law. Are you thinking of living with us, too ?
MARCELLE. I might.
                            They dance up c.
Dear Jacques, how kind you are to a lonely woman.
JACQUES. Lonely, until your next marriage.
                            They dance down c.
MARCELLE. I doubt if there'll be a next marriage.
JACQUES. Do you expect me to believe that ?
MARCELLE. There's no need for me to marry again. I'm independent.
JACQUES. That'll make it easier for me to select your next husband.
MARCELLE. Do you think I'd let you choose a husband for me ?
JACQUES. I couldn't do worse than you've done for yourself. I've even got my eye on your next victim.
MARCELLE. What nationality ?
JACQUES. French.
                    The music ceases. They stop dancing.
MARCELLE. That'll make a nice change. I shall look forward to it.
JACQUES. You might even enjoy it.
MARCELLE. I wonder what I should do if I married a man and discovered I liked it so much I wanted to stay married to him for ever ?
JACQUES [*bowing and kissing her hand*] Give him all your heart and don't let him get away.
                    The music of No. 27 is repeated.
        JACQUES *exits to the house.* MARCELLE *turns towards the tent* L.
        ANGY *enters hurriedly from the tent.*
MARCELLE. Why do you look so unhappy, Angy ? Aren't you enjoying your party ?
ANGY [*moving* LC] Why do they always have to play that tune ?
MARCELLE [*crossing to Angy*] But you liked it on the ship. You danced to it, remember ?
ANGY. Years ago.
MARCELLE. Two weeks ago.
ANGY. Where's Jacques ? I want him.
MARCELLE. Is it really Jacques you want, Angy ?
ANGY. He's my fiancé.
MARCELLE. You're quite sure you're in love with him ?
ANGY. A girl doesn't say she'll marry a man unless she thinks she's sure.
MARCELLE. Perhaps you should think again. I believe you're in love with . . .
ANGY. No !
MARCELLE. In love with Paris.
ANGY. What's wrong about that ?
MARCELLE. Sometimes when a girl loves something she can't get unless a man gives it to her, she believes she's in love with the man.
ANGY. I wouldn't be so insincere.
MARCELLE. Angy, when did you first fall in love with Dix ?
                        They sit on the garden seat LC.
ANGY. We became engaged the night after he got his job in the Paris office.
MARCELLE. And for sixteen months you dreamed of marrying him and living with him *in Paris.*

SCENE 5] WEDDING IN PARIS 53

ANGY. But it's not the same with Jacques. He loves me desperately.
MARCELLE. Angy, tell me something. Isn't there someone else of whom you think sometimes when you dream?
ANGY. If you're thinking of whom I think you're thinking, I prefer never to think of him again.

            PAUL *enters from the house.*

PAUL [*crossing to* C] Hello, there.

            ANGY *rises and moves down* L.

MARCELLE [*rising and moving to* L *of Paul*] Oh, what a *surprise*.
PAUL. Surprise? The invitation said half-past nine.
ANGY [*moving* LC] You didn't tell me you'd invited Mr Chandler.
MARCELLE. Isn't it lovely he was able to come? You can never be sure of newspaper reporters, like doctors or firemen. Oh, heavens! I've promised this dance—you two children amuse yourselves.

            MARCELLE *exits quickly to the tent. The music continues. For a few seconds,* PAUL *and* ANGY *regard each other in silence. When they begin to speak, they are self-conscious, their voices stilted.*

PAUL. Still enjoying the sights of Paris?
ANGY. Very much. When you see the great monuments of art and history, it makes you stop and think.
PAUL. What about?
ANGY. Eternal things like—like . . .
PAUL. Love?
ANGY [*moving* L] Oh, nothing so superficial.
PAUL. My mistake.
ANGY [*moving above the seat to* R *of it*] Love's an illusion—like wit and charm and beauty.
PAUL. Fine old Hitchemup philosophy, huh?
ANGY [*moving to* L *of him*] On the contrary, I learned it in Paris.
PAUL. I'm sorry. There are better things to be learned here.
ANGY. Someone should have told me.
PAUL. Someone wanted to.
ANGY [*flustered*] I've got to go and help Marcelle. Please excuse me. [*She scurries towards the tent*]

      REPRISE   No. 27a
   "IT ONLY TOOK A MOMENT"
       PAUL

PAUL.   It only took a moment to fall in love with you,

          ANGY *pauses, turns, and takes a step towards Paul.*

I saw you for a moment and then I knew,
There comes to perfect strangers
A spark we can't define,
I loved you from the moment your eyes met mine.
What happens now? Who can foresee?
Yet while you are here with me,
Let's live this precious moment

          ANGY *crosses slowly to Paul.*

Before it disappears.
If we can take our fill of
The thrill of this moment,
Perhaps this precious moment
Will last for years.

          At the end of the song they are close together.

JACQUES [*off* R ; *calling*] Angy.

ANGY *and* PAUL *are shocked out of their rapt contemplation of each other.*

JACQUES *enters from the house* R.

[*As he enters*] Angy. Look who's here. [*He moves* C]

DIX *enters from the house* R *and crosses to* RC.

ANGY [*shocked*]   Dix!   How did you get here ?   [*She does not go to Dix, but stands frozen, not daring to look at Paul*]

PAUL *backs a few steps up* LC.

JACQUES [*to* ANGY] What kind of cable was that to send a fellow who's been waiting almost two years for you ?
PAUL.   Cable ?   Where to ?

No-one heeds Paul's question.

ANGY [*crossing to* L *of Jacques*] All I said was I didn't want to marry him in his mother's backyard or ever. That's not an insult, it's the truth.
JACQUES.   His mother forgives you.   [*To Dix*]   Doesn't she ?
DIX [*sullenly*]   Yeah.
JACQUES. She told him not to take you too seriously, so he hopped on the first plane. [*To Dix*] Didn't you ?
DIX [*sullenly*]   Yeah.
JACQUES. You've misjudged him, Angy. He's far more romantic than you think. [*To Dix*] Aren't you ?
DIX.   Yeah.

MARCELLE *enters from the tent.*

MARCELLE [*astonished*]   Mr Aiken!   [*She crosses to* L *of Angy*]   I thought you went away.
JACQUES.   He came back.
MARCELLE.   For Angy's engagement party ?   [*She takes Angy's left arm to pull her away*]
JACQUES [*taking Angy's right arm and pulling her back*] For his own engagement party. This young man has flown the Atlantic to say if Angy still wants to marry him in Paris, he doesn't mind.
PAUL [*moving to* L *of Marcelle*]   Without banana pie!   Won't his mother be disappointed ?
ANGY.   Why do you always have to mix yourself up in my affairs ?
DIX.   Angy, has that guy been annoying you again ?
ANGY.   I only met him *once*.   Accidentally.
PAUL. Catastrophically, I'd call it. We agreed to differ on a matter of nakedness. [*He circles the seat, watching the others*]
DIX.   What!
JACQUES.   What ?
MARCELLE. Oh! [*To Paul*] Don't you think you should ask her to marry you at once ? [*She draws Angy towards Paul*]
JACQUES [*pulling Angy back*] Marcelle, are you deliberately trying to disillusion this romantic young lover ?
MARCELLE. As usual, you are blind to everything but your own selfish convenience. [*She moves below the seat*]
JACQUES [*following Marcelle*]   But these young people trust me implicitly—[*to Dix*] don't you ?
DIX.   Yeah.
JACQUES [*to Marcelle*]   You see.
MARCELLE.   I see.
PAUL [*moving to* R *of Jacques and slapping him on the arm*] Say, what are you ? The third party in the marriage ?
JACQUES.   Yes, no, no.   I am an old friend of the family.
PAUL.   I thought you only met Miss Dobson on the ship.
JACQUES.   We have also met once or twice since.

SCENE 5   WEDDING IN PARIS   55

PAUL. So you're the one who's been showing her all the great monuments of art and history.   MUSIC
MARCELLE. It must have been a fascinating experience. [*She sits on the garden seat* LC *at the left end*]
JACQUES. Yes, culturally.
            MARCELLE *pulls* JACQUES *down on to the seat* R *of her.*
PAUL. But when you'd had enough culture, you called the old fiancé back, huh?
ANGY. It was my cable brought Dix back here.
PAUL. I doubt that.
ANGY. Nobody asked your opinion.
MARCELLE. That doesn't stop him from having one.
PAUL. What's been going on since—[*he indicates Dix*] Romeo——
            DIX *reacts.*
—was shipped back to Saskatchewan?
ANGY. That's a question I'm proud to answer. Jacques is now my fiancé.
            JACQUES' *reaction is pained and silent.*
DIX. Huh!
PAUL. You're engaged to *him* now?
ANGY. That's the meaning of " fiancé " in English as well as French.
            PAUL *crosses to the tent to exit, but is stopped by Dix's line.*
DIX [*coming to*] Then why did Monsieur Devallée phone me to come back?
ANGY. He did?
DIX. I'm telling you he did. He told me I could have an even better job if I came back and married you.
            There is a sudden silence while JACQUES *registers his exasperation with Dix.* MARCELLE *laughs.* ANGY *gives a quick look at Jacques, then moves to* L *of Dix.*
ANGY. You're not a man—you're a puppet of International Grain and Cereal.
DIX. You've said something you'll regret.
ANGY. I'll regret nothing. I've tried to be loyal. I tried not to mind when you wanted me to go home without even tasting a snail—but when you tried to cheat me out of a holiday in Paris . . . Was that love? Was that loyalty? [*She appeals to the others*] Would *you* marry him?
DIX. The minute your foot touched French soil you began acting like the dame of the camellias. You've become a flaming example of European depravity. I hope my mother never learns the truth.
            DIX, *with dignity, exits to the house.*
PAUL. Spoken like the hero of a schoolgirl's dream. Consider what you're losing, Angy. [*He crosses above Angy and moves down* R]
ANGY [*running to Jacques*] But look what I've found.
MARCELLE [*pushing Jacques to his feet*] Go on, dear.
JACQUES [*taking Angy by the shoulders*] An illusion already fading.
ANGY. No! We can *make* it last.
JACQUES. My little one, you are very sweet. [*He leads her* C] I adore you but I cannot allow you to make such a sacrifice.
MARCELLE. Neither can Paul.
PAUL. Let me speak for myself.
MARCELLE. I don't trust you. [*She rises*] You're too much in love to control your emotions.
JACQUES. So I've noticed. [*He crosses to Paul*] I'm delighted to meet you again; we've got a vacancy in our office and you're just the man for the job.
MARCELLE [*crossing to* L *of Jacques*] How generous, Jacques, and how like you.
PAUL. I wouldn't ask you for a job.
MARCELLE. It's not only the job he's offering you. It's Angy . . .
ANGY [*crossing to* L *of Marcelle*] Offering me! What does he think I am, a prize calf at an auction?
PAUL. Don't worry, I'm not bidding. Love's not enough. You've got to be rich to win the Saskatchewan prize. Let me congratulate you, Angy. Tough luck, Marcelle. Good-bye.

PAUL *exits to the house.* JACQUES *follows him to the door.* [MUSIC]

MARCELLE. It's what I've always said, you can never trust the newspapers.
ANGY [*moving to the seat* LC] I'd have trusted him—but it's too late—he's walked out on me. [*She sits on the seat*] And Dix has gone—and my girlhood's gone.
JACQUES. It has!

MARCELLE *crosses and sits* L *of Angy on the seat.* JACQUES *crosses to* R *of the seat.*

ANGY. Of course it has. I'm a flagrant example of European depravity. There's nothing for me now but to go back and be an old maid in Saskatchewan. [*She weeps*]
JACQUES [*sitting* R *of Angy and taking her hand*] Poor little Angy.
MARCELLE. We can't allow that.
JACQUES. Something has to be done.
MARCELLE [*rising; perplexed*] What?

The lights BLACK-OUT *as—*

[LIGHTING CUE 19]

the RUNNING TABS *close*

SCENE 6

Outside the Cathedral, Paris

The scene is a gauze with a black backing depicting the outside of the Cathedral.

FINALE. ACT II [No. 28]

CHORUS

When the RUNNING TABS *open, the* WEDDING GUESTS *enter and sing the reprises. With them are* MRS PILCHARD *and the* REPORTERS.

CHORUS.   How do I know it's love?
             I must be sure it's love.
             Will someone come to guide me,
             My dream appear beside me?
             Maybe I'll see a sign,
             Shine like a star from above,
             Although I know my heart says it's so
             How do I know it's love?

             I have nothing to declare,
             Nothing to declare but love.
             I have nothing to declare,
             Nothing to declare but love.
             If you could search my heart,
             My love you'll find in there.
             I have nothing to declare,
             Nothing to declare but love.
             Nothing, nothing, nothing, nothing, nothing
             To declare but love.
             Nothing to declare but love.

             The young in heart are always young,
             Be young in heart and you'll be young.
             The Winter comes when birds take wing,
             But if there's sunshine in your heart, it's always Spring.
             Though Autumn leaves must fall some day,
             Love treats September just like May.

SCENE 7 — WEDDING IN PARIS

The BLACK BACKING *rises*

Time doesn't matter when you hear a love song sung,
The young in heart are always young.

The lights come up behind the gauze.

LIGHTING CUE 20

The music continues

The GAUZE *rises*

SCENE 7

Inside the Cathedral, Paris

There is an altar back C, *flanked by candelabra.*
When the GAUZE *rises,* JACQUES *and* MARCELLE *are kneeling at the altar, with their backs to the audience, in front of the* CLERGYMAN. MARCELLE *is shrouded in layers of lace and tulle.* ANGY, *a maid of honour, is in a bouffant gown and an enormous hat. Neither Marcelle nor Angy should be at first recognized by the audience or Paul. The* DANCERS *are there as bridesmaids. The* GUESTS *move up and take their places* R *and* L, *with their backs to the audience. The* REPORTERS *are down* L.

CHORUS. Here are the bride and the bridegroom,
Happy the day for bride and bridegroom,
God speed their way for every day,
And let's say, Amen.

PAUL *enters down* L. *The* CLERGYMAN *takes on the rhythm of the marriage service.*

CLERGYMAN. Do you, Jacques Jean Christophe Rolande Olivier Hilaire Marie Devallée, take this woman to be your lawful wedded wife?
JACQUES. I do.
CLERGYMAN. Do you . . . ?

The Clergyman's voice is drowned out by the REPORTERS.

BERMAN [*moving to* R *of Paul*] Just in time for the kill.
PAUL. I hate weddings.
FRISCH [*moving to* L *of Paul*] Why did you come?
PAUL. Orders from the front office. Devallée called up the boss and asked that Paul Chandler personally cover the ceremony.

There are murmurs of "Shh, shh" from some of the GUESTS.

ARCHER. Did you see my Sunday story? She says that this time . . .
GUESTS [*ad lib.*] Sh-shh! Silence, Messieurs.

The REPORTERS *are silent. The* CLERGYMAN'S *voice is heard.*

CLERGYMAN. I now pronounce you man and wife.

MARCELLE *and* JACQUES *rise.* MARCELLE *raises her veil and* JACQUES *embraces her. The bridal group turn and face front.* PAUL *sees Angy and gasps with astonishment.*

PAUL. Angy! [*He moves towards her*]
ANGY [*moving towards Paul*] Paul!
PAUL. I've got to talk to you.
ANGY. Be quiet, please. You're at a wedding.

PAUL, *instead of returning humbly to his place, takes Angy in his arms.* ANGY *accepts.*

PAUL. A wedding in Paris—how about it, Angy?
ANGY. Yes.

MELOS

THE COMPANY

> PAUL *and* ANGY *clasp each other.* MARCELLE, JACQUES, *and the* GUESTS *come downstage. During the singing* ANGY *runs to* JACQUES. *He looks at* MARCELLE, *who nods, then he kisses* ANGY *on the forehead.*

COMPANY.
A wedding in Paris, she's going to be married,
And over a threshold she's going to be carried,
The happiest bride you will see,
Ah, oui, oui, oui,
A wedding in Paris there'll be.

> ANGY *runs to* PAUL. *The two couples embrace as the singing ends and—*
>
> *the* CURTAIN *falls*

FURNITURE AND PROPERTY PLOT

ACT I

Scene 1

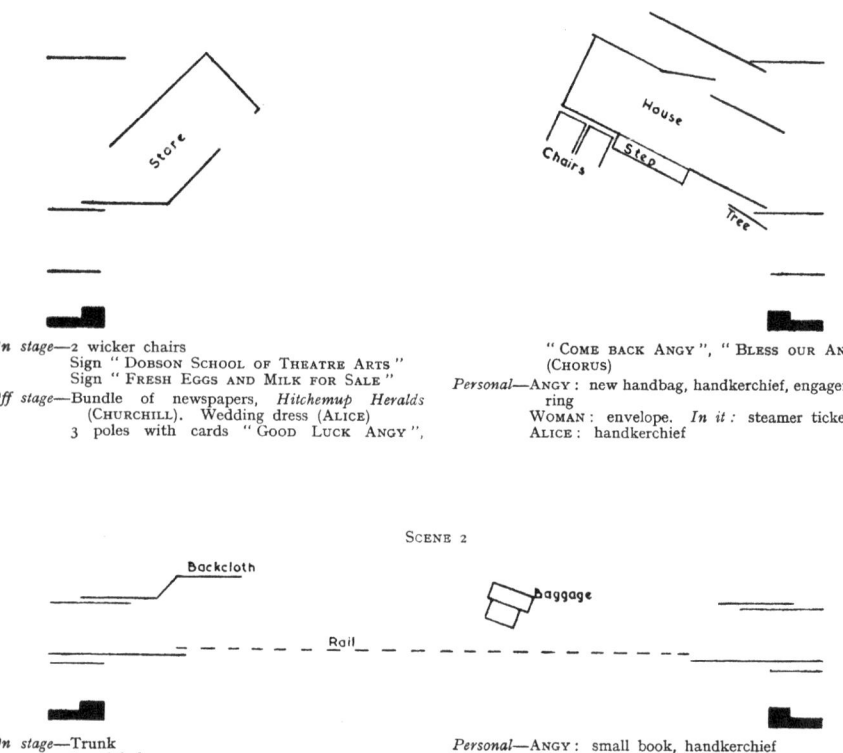

On stage—2 wicker chairs
  Sign " DOBSON SCHOOL OF THEATRE ARTS "
  Sign " FRESH EGGS AND MILK FOR SALE "
Off stage—Bundle of newspapers, *Hitchemup Heralds* (CHURCHILL). Wedding dress (ALICE)
  3 poles with cards " GOOD LUCK ANGY ", " COME BACK ANGY ", " BLESS OUR ANGY " (CHORUS)
Personal—ANGY: new handbag, handkerchief, engagement ring
  WOMAN: envelope. *In it:* steamer ticket
  ALICE: handkerchief

Scene 2

On stage—Trunk
  Small bale
Personal—ANGY: small book, handkerchief
  PAUL: visiting card

WEDDING IN PARIS

Scene 3

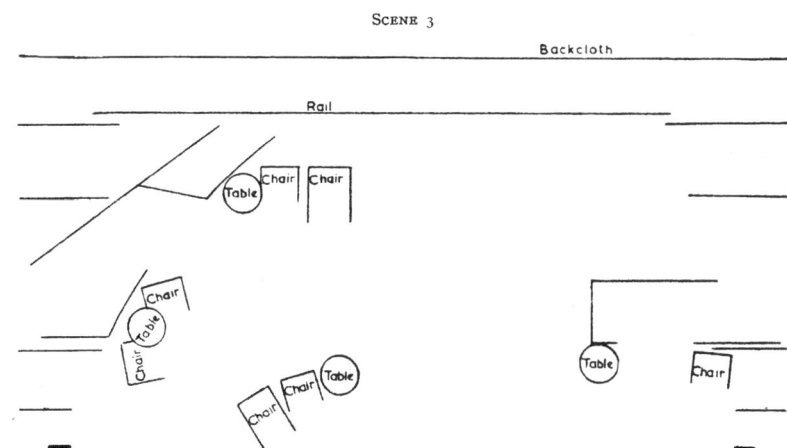

On stage—3 tables. *On them :* glasses, ashtrays
    4 chairs
    1 lounge chair with leg rest. *On it :* cushion
    2 lounge chairs. *On them :* cushions
    1 small table. *On it :* ashtray
    2 sunshades on stands
    Lifebelts and flags as dressing
Off stage—Newspaper (JACQUES)
    Tray and napkin (CHIEF STEWARD)

Tray. *On it :* bottle of champagne in cooler, 2 champagne glasses (2ND STEWARD)
Marcelle's handy-bag and magazine (CHIEF STEWARD)
Tray. *On it :* brandy and soda, chit pad and pencil (2ND STEWARD)
Tray. *On it :* champagne glass (CHIEF STEWARD)
Personal—JACQUES : case with cigarettes, lighter
    CHIEF STEWARD : passenger list

Scene 4

No properties

Scene 5

On stage—Table (R). *On it :* 3 drinks
    3 chairs (at table R)
    Table (L). *On it :* glass with whisky and soda
    2 chairs (at table L)
    Fairy lights

Off stage—Glass of whisky and soda (CHIEF STEWARD)
    Glass of Green Chartreuse (CHIEF STEWARD)
    Glass of whisky and soda (CHIEF STEWARD)
Personal—CHIEF STEWARD : tray, napkin, chit pad, pencil
    ANGY : handkerchief

Scene 6

Personal—JACQUES : handkerchief

WEDDING IN PARIS

SCENE 7

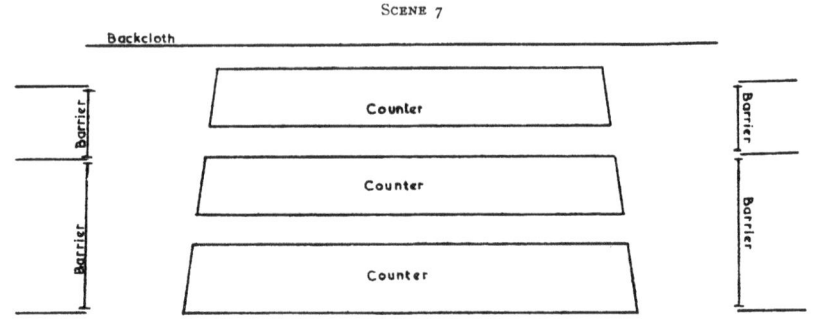

On stage—3 rostrum counters
    Barriers
    Lamp-posts with travel posters
    Pendant signs with letters
Off stage—Suitcases. *In them:* garments (PASSENGERS)
    Luggage (PORTERS)

Jacques' overcoat and gloves (CHIEF STEWARD)
Trolley. *On it:* Marcelle's luggage (PORTER)
    Angy's case, Paul's case (PORTER)
Personal—CUSTOMS OFFICERS: sticks of chalk
    JACQUES: franc notes

ACT II

SCENE 1

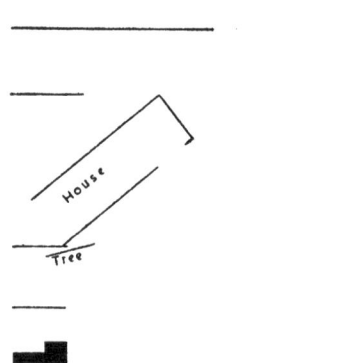
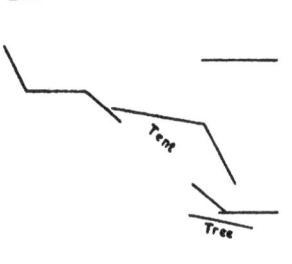

On stage—Long garden seat* (RC)
    Garden table* (LC). *On it:* ashtray
    2 garden chairs* (LC)
Off stage—Sun glasses, cameras, guide books, maps (TOURISTS)
    Basket of red roses (MARCELLE)

6 notebooks and pencils (REPORTERS)
Spray of orchids (MARCELLE)
Bouquet of roses (PAUL)
Personal—GUIDE: stick
    JACQUES: case with cigarettes, lighter
* *Not shown on the plan*

WEDDING IN PARIS 63

SCENE 2

Tourist properties as previous scene

SCENE 3

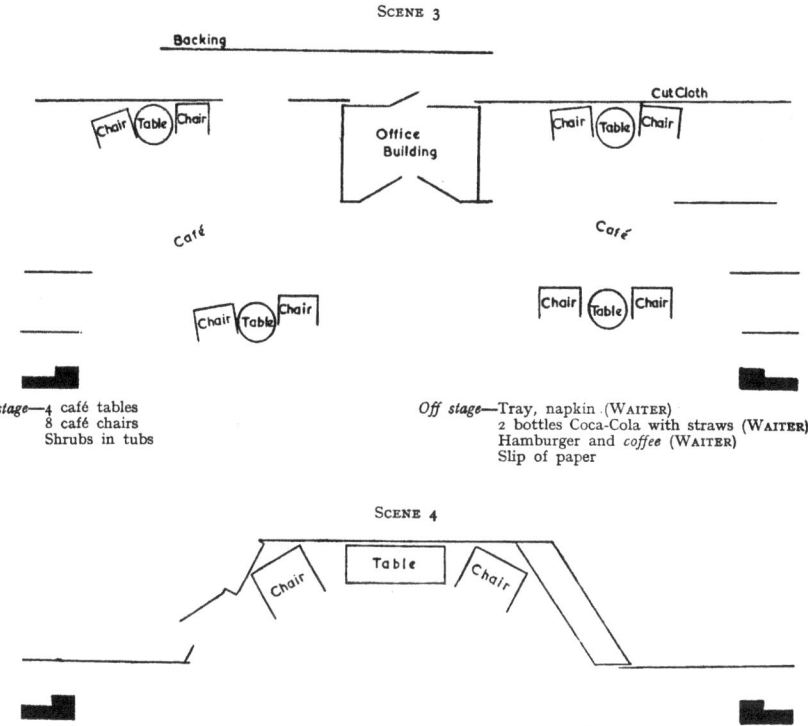

On stage—4 café tables
   8 café chairs
   Shrubs in tubs

Off stage—Tray, napkin (WAITER)
   2 bottles Coca-Cola with straws (WAITER)
   Hamburger and *coffee* (WAITER)
   Slip of paper

SCENE 4

On stage—2 armchairs. *On them :* cushions
   Console table. *On it :* cigarette lighter, tray with decanter of sherry and two glasses

Small carpet
On ledge L: telephone, ashtray, globe

SCENE 5

On stage—Garden seat
   Tent-piece L
   Chinese lanterns

SCENE 6

No properties

Scene 7

```
            Backcloth
    ─────────────────────
   /                         ┌─────────┐                              ─
  /                           │  Altar  │                               \
                              └─────────┘                                \
              Candelabrum              Candelabrum
───                                                                   ───

           Candelabrum                    Candelabrum
───                                                                   ───

         Candelabrum                       Candelabrum


                              Gauze
───  ──  ──  ──  ──  ──  ──  ──  ──  ──  ──  ──                       ───


───                                                                   ───

■▄                                                                    ▄■
```

On stage—Altar
          Candelabra

Off stage—Bride's bouquet (MARCELLE)
          Bridesmaid's posies (DANCERS)

LIGHTING PLOT

ACT I SCENE 1 Exterior. Morning
Property fittings required—none
    THE MAIN ACTING AREAS ARE—the whole stage
To open. Effect of bright morning sunshine
Cue 1   As RUNNING TABS close at end of Scene 1 (page 5)
      Quick dim to BLACK-OUT
Cue 2   When RUNNING TABS are closed   (page 5)
      Bring in F.O.H. lights

ACT I SCENE 2 Exterior. Daytime
Property fittings required—none
    THE MAIN ACTING AREA IS—down C
To open: F.O.H. spots focused C
      Float and Number 1 batten
Cue 3   Song " The French Lesson "   (page 9)
      Fade float and batten
Cue 4   At end of song   (page 10)
      Snap BLACK-OUT
Cue 5   When the RUNNING TABS are closed   (page 10)
      Bring up F.O.H. lights
Cue 6   When the RUNNING TABS open   (page 10)
      Bring up Stage Lights

ACT I SCENE 3 Exterior. Morning
Property fittings required—none
    THE MAIN ACTING AREAS ARE—the whole stage
To open: Effect of bright sunshine
Cue 7   Song " The Young in Heart "   (page 15)
      Check lights to ¾
Cue 8   At end of song   (page 16)
      Snap BLACK-OUT
Cue 9   When the RUNNING TABS are closed   (page 16)
      Bring up F.O.H. lights
Cue 10   At end of song   (page 17)
      Snap BLACK-OUT

ACT I SCENE 4 Exterior. Night
Property fittings required—none
    THE MAIN ACTING AREA IS—down C
To open: F.O.H. spots focused C
      Blue in float and Number 1 batten
Cue 11   At end of scene   (page 18)
      Quick dim to BLACK-OUT
Cue 12   When the RUNNING TABS are closed   (page 18)
      Bring up F.O.H. lights
Cue 13   At end of song   (page 18)
      Quick dim to BLACK-OUT

ACT I SCENE 5 Exterior. Night
Property fittings required—fairy lights (practical)
    THE MAIN ACTING AREAS ARE—the whole stage
To open: Effect of bright moonlight
      Fairy lights lit
No cues

ACT I SCENE 6 Exterior. Night
The lighting from the previous scene stands
Cue 14   At end of scene   (page 25)
      Quick dim to BLACK-OUT

ACT I SCENE 7 Interior. Afternoon
Property fittings required—none
    THE MAIN ACTING AREAS ARE—the whole stage
To open: Effect of bright sunlight
Cue 15   As FRONT-CLOTH rises   (page 25)
      Bring up lights

ACT II SCENE 1 Exterior. Morning
Property fittings required—none
    THE MAIN ACTING AREAS ARE—the whole stage
To open: Effect of bright sunshine
Cue 16   At end of scene   (page 41)
      Quick dim to BLACK-OUT

ACT II SCENE 2 Exterior. Daytime
To open: F.O.H. lights
      Float and Number 1 batten
No cues

ACT II SCENE 3 Exterior. Daytime
To open: Effect of bright sunshine
Cue 17   At end of scene   (page 47)
      Quick dim to BLACK-OUT

ACT II SCENE 4 Interior
To open: F.O.H. lights
      Float and Number 1 batten
Cue 18   At end of scene   (page 50)
      Quick dim to BLACK-OUT

ACT II SCENE 5 Exterior. Evening
Property fittings required—Chinese lanterns
    THE MAIN ACTING AREAS ARE—the whole stage
To open: Effect of bright moonlight
      Chinese lanterns lit
      Floods in house R and tent L
Cue 19   At end of scene   (page 56)
      Quick dim to BLACK-OUT

ACT II SCENE 6 Exterior
To open: Front of gauze lighting
No cues

ACT II SCENE 7 Interior
Property fittings required—6 candelabra (practical)
To open: Effect of candlelight
      Candelabra lit
Cue 20   When BLACK BACKING rises   (page 57)
      Bring up lighting as above

Act I Scene 1

Act I Scenes 2 and 4

Act I Scenes 3 and 5

To face p. 66—Wedding in Paris

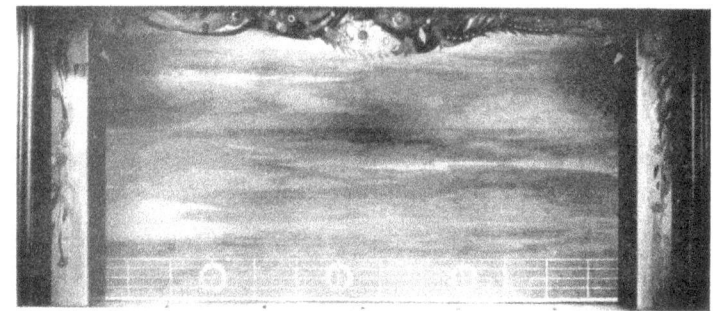

Act I Scene 6

Act I Scene 7

Act II Scenes 1 and 5

Act II Scene 2

Act II Scene 3

Act II Scene 4

Act II Scene 6

Act II Scene 7